MOVED BY
COMPASSION

MOVED BY COMPASSION

MOBILIZING YOUR LOCAL CHURCH
TO TRANSFORM YOUR CITY

JAMIE LINDSAY

ANOINTED
PUBLISHING

Printed in the United States of America
First Printing, 2020

ISBN 979-85771988-7-9

Anointed Publishing
An imprint of Limitless, LLC
PO Box 509
Carleton, MI 48117

Neither the author nor the publisher assumes any responsibility for errors,
omissions, or contrary interpretations of the subject matter herein. Any
perceived slight of any individual or organization is purely unintentional.
Some of the events described happened as related, others were expanded
and changed. The names and other identifying characteristics of the
persons included in this book have been changed. Throughout this book
I have used examples from many of my clients' personal lives and personal
stories. However, to ensure privacy and confidentiality I have changed
some of their names and some of the details of their experience.
All of the personal examples of my own life have not been altered.

Bible Translations and Reference Key

Abbreviation	Translation
AMP	Amplified Bible
CEB	Common English Bible
CEV	Contemporary English Version
CJB	Complete Jewish Bible
ESV	English Standard Version
KJV	King James Version
MSG	The Message
NIV	New International Version
NLT	New Living Translation
Voice	The Voice
Strongs	Blue Letter Bible. (n.d.). Retrieved from https://www.blueletterbible.org/.
	Strong, J. (1890). *Strong's exhaustive concordance of the Bible.* Abingdon Press.

Table of Contents

Jesus, I give to you all that I am and all that I have.

Acknowledgements

Writing my first book was no easy task. It was a labor of love to say the least. However, I would have never entertained the idea of writing a book without the people in my life who loved me, supported me, believed in me, and prayed for me.

To my husband, Rob, and our girls, Ava and Ella, I know you have sacrificed so much over the years as I worked towards my goals and set out on this journey to live out God's purpose for my life. I love you all so much and I never take for granted all you have done to help me get this book published.

To my mother, Lisa, thank you for working so hard and showing me what it means to approach life with determination, grit, and perseverance. To my dad, Jeff, thank you for loving me and being my dad because you chose to be. It means so much to me. It is because of this choice I have you in my life and got the greatest nana and papa anyone could have asked for. Nana and Papa, I can't wait to see you in Heaven someday. Nana, I know you will have some delicious baked goods of some sort ready to celebrate my entry into Heaven, and Papa you will greet me with a smile and with that laugh I miss so much now. Together, you were my grand prize in life. I am who I am today because of your prayers, guidance, and unconditional love.

Thank you to Josh, Ashley, Rob, Brooke, Taylor, Dalton, Alexia, Tyler, Ayden, and Scott for being you and being part of my tribe. I love you all so much!

To my best friends, Amy and Kathy: girls, I couldn't have done this without you. You were my shoulder to cry on and the coaches I needed to keep me going forward. I can not express to you how much you both mean to me. Every tribe needs a head council and you are mine. Aunt Cindi, so much time we spent on the phone talking about all the things God has put in my heart about His purpose for my life. You have always been my biggest cheerleader. You and Uncle Dave remind me of how important it is to make your family a priority. You have kept me grounded. Thank you!

To my coach and mentor, Schlyce Jimenez, I really, truly could not have gotten this far without you pushing me to my limits. You helped me get over the lies I was believing about myself and get into alignment with God's truth for my life. I will forever be grateful. You also gave me the opportunity to be in community with my fellow world changers. *Emergers*, I love you!

To my awesome small group, Jacob, Kellie, Dan, Deb, Dee, Brad, and Kathy, I love you all so much! Thank you for the amazing conversations that have not only helped me with this message God placed in my heart, but helped me grow in my intimacy with the Lord. These friendships are nothing short of a sovereign blessing from God. Thank you!

Jane Martin and Jane Severson, thank you for pushing me to go back to school, challenging me when you knew I wasn't working at my potential, and giving me the opportunity to learn from you. You both are amazing, talented, intelligent women and I am better for knowing you.

Professor Bryan Alfaro, thank you for your patience and expertise in editing this book. You have taught me how to be a better writer and to express my thoughts in a way I could impact those I am writing to. Thank you for the countless hours you have spent helping me make my first book a reality. There are so many others who have been part of my journey. You all know who you are. You have a special place in my heart.

Preface

♥

"What Would Happen If The Church Tithed?" was the title of an article in *Relevant Magazine* written by Mike Holmes. Mr. Holmes discussed if church members faithfully gave their 10%, it would generate an additional $165 billion. He went on to say that that would be more than enough to end world hunger, illiteracy, the unclean water crisis, and it would be enough to fund overseas mission work with a hefty $100 billion left over for the church to use to expand ministries. This would be a dream come true to a world that is in such dire straits as we are, right?

We live in a time in which it can feel as if our society is a train moving at full speed ahead towards a cliff. Those who still watch the news are bombarded with stories related to mass shootings, health care reform, and political scandals. For people like myself, and maybe you who are reading this book, it can feel overwhelming. Not to mention that mental health issues like increased stress levels, depression, and suicide are higher than ever before. Despite our ability to be more connected than any other generation, our relationships and social interactions are deteriorating and many people feel isolated. We also live in one of the sickest times in our history, as more people are plagued with disease. And, what's worse? The leading causes of diseases are preventable. Many people feel spiritually, emotionally, and physically bankrupt. For those of us working in public health or the healthcare system, we see how these things are all working together (but against us) to create one giant healthcare crisis.

How is this all connected to Mr. Holmes' article? I love that he brought generosity to the forefront of people's minds. However, it spurred a thought for me that goes one step further: Even if everyone gave and the Church had access to the $165 billion, would they steward the money in the ways Holmes suggested? Or, would those billions of dollars stay internally within the organization to purchase new buildings, lighting systems, and production studios? Perhaps a small percentage of it would actually go to improving the lives of the needy? The U.S. Census Bureau reported in 2017 that there are more than 39 million people just in the United States who are living in poverty. However, according to Pew Research Center's Religious Landscape Study, there are more than 93 million people in the United States who identify both as Christian and as attending services at least once a week. That is 2.4 Christians for every one person living in poverty. What if we actually put giving *and* action to the test? What if the Church cared deeply for their community and was courageously generous to those living in poverty in order to build the Kingdom of God here on Earth? This is where the rubber meets the road, so to speak. If people gave generously to their church organizations and the church organizations invested financial resources and worked to mobilize their congregants, the underlying issue of poverty could be resolved.

How can anyone or a few persons change all that is wrong with the world? The good news is that one person, Jesus, has died so that we might live and that no matter how bad things get—He has already overcome this world. Any struggle that we experience today, there is a victory to be had. For those of us who are believers in Jesus Christ, this is the fundamental core of our faith. People are in desperate need of this hope in their life. However, in the eyes of some, the Church has become trivial in today's world. For many Christians these days, attending church has become merely a "check the box" on Sunday morning without a focus on really developing a deep unshakeable faith. The Church has also become irrelevant to those on the outside looking in. Much of the world rejects us because they view us as a cultish social club full of bigots. I know that sounds harsh, but that is the reality of the perception of many people who do not accept the Christian faith. There was a point in time when the Church was relevant. The Body of Christ was the solution to society's problems. In fact, the first hospitals and orphanages were started and managed by Christian churches. Charitable acts and caring for the sick and poor used to be a central part of our mission. Churches were a cornerstone for families and communities. James 1:27 tells us a "pure and unblemished religion [as it is expressed in outward acts] in the sight of our God and Father is this: to visit and look after the fatherless and the widows in their distress, and to keep oneself uncontaminated by the [secular] world" (AMP).

Eradicating poverty and addressing the underlying issues contributing to poverty is a difficult task. Nevertheless, there are truths found in the Bible that provide answers for meeting all of these needs but we, the Church, have been complacent for too long.

We have been content to take a back seat and have relinquished this responsibility for caring for the needy to the government through assistance programs and anyone else but us. This book focuses on meeting practical needs of those living in poverty because, as Paul said, we need to be "all things to all people" (1 Cor. 9:22 NIV).

For all these problems that influence the health of individuals, the Church and the church organization could be and should be the answer to all of them. Did you know that just the presence of hope can lower blood pressure and strengthen the immune system? This is something that has been well studied in science. On the other hand, compassion does hope one better. Compassion is actually good for our health and the health of others around us. We are physiologically and cognitively at our best when we feel compassion for others. This is something we anecdotally can relate to, but science also demonstrates this. When we show compassion towards others, we inspire them to be open to new possibilities and ideas.

Compassion is a word that we use to describe a feeling of concern or love for others. Compassion is the propensity towards empathy which allows us to connect with the experiences and suffering of others. The word *compassion* appears 71 times in 67 verses in the Bible. In the Old Testament, the word *r âcham* (Strong H3755) is used to describe God's love, tenderness, and mercy for his people. However, when we see this word in connection with Jesus, we see a different p hrase t o d escribe h is c ompassion. I n t he K ing J ames Version, the phrase is translated as he was "moved by compassion" or *splagchnizomai* (Strong G4697). In fact, this phrase that the apostles used to describe the response that Jesus had towards people required a new word, as one didn't exist in the Greek language. There wasn't a word that accurately described the response that Jesus felt about his people. This new phrase described a deep rooted yearning or longing towards love and mercy for those he encountered during his ministry.

Each time this phrase is used, it is in the context of Jesus observing a person's suffering followed by actions in response to their suffering . Pastor Charles Sprugeon described Jesus' response like this, "I suppose that when our Savior looked upon certain sights, those who watched Him closely perceived that His internal agitation was very great, His emotions were very deep, and then His face betrayed it, His eyes gushed like founts with tears, and you saw that His big heart was ready to burst with pity for the sorrow upon which his eyes were gazing. He was *moved with compassion*. His whole nature was agitated with commiseration for the sufferers before him." Jesus didn't just empathize with those who were suffering, He experienced a deep, profound reaction that moved Him to the point of action. It is this same compassion for humanity that compelled Jesus to the ultimate act of laying down his life for our salvation.

My prayer as I write this book is to inspire church leaders to reconnect with the heart of Jesus for people so that they are compelled to address the effects of poverty in their community by developing outreach programs that have a measurable impact and saturates their community with the Good News. We live in a world where it seems impossible to address issues such as poverty. It is immense to think about the number of people who are struggling just to make it day to day. In spite of this, I want to empower church leaders so that they accomplish the work God has assigned them to do within their community and the vision God has given them for their church so that they can be faithful in fulfilling the Kingdom assignment God has for them to reach the lost. In order to do this, however, we have to model our ministry like Jesus'. We need to develop a heart that is so affected by the love, mercy, and tenderness that the Father has for people, that we are then moved to action. This means, we need to first seek the Lord and ask Him to change our hearts and give us eyes to see what He sees. Then, to accomplish the work of this ministry, we need to question the status quo of the modern church and get back to the basics. We may need to question our attitudes, mindsets, and practices as they relate to caring for the poor and managing money.

We are in a time where the world is in desperate need of love. It is through His Church the people can experience the transforming and radical love that Jesus has for them.

Chapter 1

"If you dislike change, you're going to dislike irrelevance even more"
- General Eric Shinseki

It was a gloomy winter day when I arrived at work. I parked in the lot and began walking toward the building when a call came in. The call was from one of the congregants at my church. He was calling to let me know that he and his family were being evicted on that following Monday. They were in the final stages of the eviction process, which meant that the police department would come to their home, his family would be allowed to take only what they could carry, and they would be forced to vacate the premises. All of their belongings, such as photos, clothes, furniture, dishes, and even what food they had, would be confiscated.

He was, as you can imagine, frantic about what he would do should they actually be evicted from their home. He was calling me for help as I, along with my husband, were the newly appointed directors of the Outreach Department. Benevolence, or charitable giving, fell under our purview. I began to ask him questions about what happened, how did this happen, and what money did he have on hand (which wasn't much) to help cover the debt. Next, I did what I could to help him calm down for a moment, prayed with him, and said that I would see what I could do to help and would call him later. But, the truth was, I had no idea how I was going to help him. Our church had never had a benevolence process. In fact, what was

1

referred to as benevolence really only referred to funeral dinners up to this point.

When I had taken this volunteer director role in my church, I started out trying to understand what resources exist in the community. This helped me meet with some of the local non-profit leaders and I began building my own network. Truth be told, I had never held any type of leadership position in a church before. While I am resourceful and determined, I really had no idea how to handle these types of situations. However, when I took the role, benevolence was one area that I knew I would need to have an infrastructure and would also challenge the perspectives of many of those on our church board and finance committee. They are all loving people who have loved and walked with the Lord for a long time. I did not doubt that they love the Lord. However, asking them to give money to people was going to be a stretch. Such spending, since it wasn't "in the budget", had to get approval from our administrative board.

I sent an email asking them to approve a request to provide financial assistance for this family in our congregation that was facing eviction. They responded by approving the request, but also stated that budgeted funds should not be used for such requests moving forward. I was taken aback by this response. To get some perspective, I reached out to one of our board members and asked him to meet me for lunch, so I could explore the reasons the board felt the way they did. The overall sentiment after that conversation was that it was the Church body, not the church organization that was responsible for meeting the needs of the people. When we ended our conversation, he said one final thought that struck me in such a way that I decided to write this book as an answer to it. He said, "I guess we need to define the roles and responsibilities of the church and of the people." When he said that, I felt like I had just been hit by a ton of bricks. It sent a shock wave into my spirit because it was then that I realized that there is a perception that there are two entities: The Church of the bible, which includes every individual who is a believer and follower of Jesus Christ, and the church organization (the legal entity referred to as the church).

I have grown up in church nearly my entire life. There were times when I would leave or not attend church regularly, but I always seemed to find my way back. And, it wasn't that I just went to church my entire life, I had only gone to one church my entire life. My perception was so narrow up to that point. I accepted the status quo as it was and didn't question it because I didn't know any differently. Over the years, I have heard many, many friends and family members talk about the church. They would say things like, "Those Christians are all hypocrites" and "All the church wants is my money." I was always defensive when I heard people say things like these because my experience was that I went to church with a lot of great people and tithing was just part of what you did because God told us to do it in Scripture. I never questioned it.

So, when my board member said those things to me at our lunch, it was like my eyes had been opened for the first time; I began to hear and see the discrepancies as it related to money and tithing. And, not only that, it was perceived as ridiculous that we would want to give money to the poor. Don't get me wrong, some of the money was used for our pastor's salary, vacation bible school, and student ministry events, but the majority of it was being spent on overhead and fellowship dinners and events that were completely facing inwards towards our congregants. Nearly none of the money was used on being charitable or reaching the lost. And, if it was, it was giving money to other organizations who did the work.

I began asking my friends who attended other churches what their process was for charitable giving. Most of them said that they used to have a food pantry or used to give more, but their tithing was down so they cut that ministry. One of my friends told me that her church used 30% of their annual budget for missions. But, when I asked her how much of that goes to the local community, she said that none of it did. Instead they send the money to a missionary in India.

What I had heard from my friends and family about the church organization began unfolding. From the perspective of unbelievers or those who have left the church, it looks like church is nothing more than a social club. You pay your dues and then you reap the benefits: free meals, fun activities for your kids, and events for holidays. Don't get me wrong; those things have a place in church culture and they do serve a purpose for investing in the congregation. The fact is that most churches have a lot of great programs and resources, but they only go as far as the four walls of their building and those events typically include regular attendees with a gentle nudge to invite friends. In fact, outreach looks more like a marketing campaign than a real investment in reaching the lost. Our cities are in poverty and oppression and our churches are having a potluck.

I recently watched an interview with a very well-known televangelist. He was being interviewed by a popular media outlet. They were asking him what he says to those who say pastors shouldn't have all the money that he has. He isn't the first televangelist or pastor to be asked that same question. People inside and outside of the church have begun to ask questions about how pastors and churches spend the money that is given to them. Many of them are being investigated for private inurement, or using church monies to benefit individuals within the organization. This can be using church monies to pay for private jets, luxury cars, and extravagant homes or vacations. There is a well-known website that looks at 501c3 charities and provides consumers a score based on how the money is used on things like missional focused activities, operational costs, and overhead. This site began because most people want to be charitable, but they want their dollars to count. Anyone can use this website to find charities that have a higher rating to select who to donate to. I often wonder how churches would fair if given the same rigorous scoring.

Why is asking how we spend money an important issue to address? I think we should ask ourselves: How does the church organization's use of money reflect who Jesus is? This is an important question to ask ourselves because we are to be His reflection. In fact, 1 John 2:6 says, "Whoever says he abides in Him ought to walk in the same way in which He walked." Are we walking the same way He did when we don't care about the struggles of others and take more than we give? So many people have been hurt by the church. Their impression of who God is has been warped by the bad behaviors occurring within His Church. When the Church is stingy, it reinforces beliefs that God doesn't care about them. When we are ungenerous with what we have, it sets in motion a belief that God is also ungenerous. When we build fancy churches with state-of-the-art lighting systems while there are people in our community who don't have enough to live on, how might that look to those on the outside? What might God think about this? Are we building God's Kingdom here on Earth where people are being released from physical, emotional, and spiritual oppression? Or, could it look like the kingdom we are building is just a castle in the middle of the ghetto?

As a church body, we must face the fact that the world thinks the Church is greedy. We can no longer hide behind John 15:18, "If the world hates you, keep in mind that it hated me first." Non-believers aren't rejecting Jesus; they are rejecting us. Even our own people are leaving the church. Doesn't it burden you that the Bride of Christ is full of self-loathing that people separate themselves from it? Not all the things that are said about the church organization and Christianity are untrue, particularly the western church. We have to acknowledge that. We can't claim persecution while our people are judgmental, critical, and lacking in compassion. We have to come to terms that how the church uses money and our biases about the poor are stumbling blocks to reaching the lost and building the Kingdom.

Jesus clearly explains what he expects of us when he says in Matthew 25:34-40, "Then the King will say to those on his right, 'Come, you who are blessed by my Father; take your inheritance, the Kingdom prepared for you since the creation of the world. For I was hungry and you gave me something to eat, I was thirsty and you gave me something to drink, I was a stranger and you invited me in, I needed clothes and you clothed me, I was sick and you looked after me, I was in prison and you came to visit me.' Then the righteous will answer him, 'Lord, when did we see you hungry and feed you, or thirsty and give you something to drink? When did we see you a stranger and invite you in, or needing clothes and clothe you? When did we see you sick or in prison and go to visit you?' The King will reply, 'Truly I tell you, whatever you did for one of the least of these brothers and sisters of mine, you did for me.'"

Jesus, as He does in many ways, flips the script on what we think God wants and asks us to not focus on the brick and mortar temple, but to honor Him, the true temple of God (John 2:19-22), through being lavishly generous to those in need. Caring for the needy is not a new attribute in God's character. In fact, throughout Scripture, God demonstrates His care for the poor by setting aside crops so that the needy will be provided for. In the Old Testament, He tells the Israelites to refrain from harvesting the edges of their fields so that there is food for the poor (Lev. 23:22). He also tells them if some of the crops fall to the ground, leave it for them as well (Lev 19:10).

I love the Body of Christ. I yearn for Her to reconnect to Jesus' heart for people. To reinstate compassion into mainstream churches so that we are no longer pulling people into the confines of our walls, but meeting people where they are. However, to do that, we have to be willing to look at ourselves honestly and be willing to do what it takes to move forward towards God's will for His Church and the lost in our communities. That means, transforming what we think we know and allowing God to reestablish His Kingdom by formulating our mindsets for how we think about church and most certainly how we think about the impoverished. We also have to be willing to connect the dots between Christian tradition and secular research and ways for approaching and addressing the problem. What I mean is that there is a ton of research on the challenges of poverty, social problems, how to address them, and also practical knowledge like change management and process measurement that could be largely useful in helping us build ministries.

My hope is that this book will help you begin to see the challenges that those living in poverty or near poverty experience, but also to help you dissect the mindsets that exist within churches that might prevent them from the inheritance that God promised us in Matthew 25:34. If we don't do something, my fear when I think of our churches is this the rest of the Matthew 25 passage, verses 41-46:

"Then the King will say to those on his left, 'Get away from me! You are under God's curse. Go into the everlasting fire prepared for the devil and his angels! I was hungry, but you did not give me anything to eat, and I was thirsty, but you did not give me anything to drink. I was a stranger, but you did not welcome me, and I was naked, but you did not give me any clothes to wear. I was sick and in jail, but you did not take care of me.' Then the people will ask, 'Lord, when did we fail to help you when you were hungry or thirsty or a stranger or naked or sick or in jail?' The King will say to them, 'Whenever you failed to help any of my people, no matter how unimportant they seemed, you failed to do it for me.' Then Jesus said, 'Those people will be punished forever. But the ones who pleased God will have eternal life.'"

Writing this book is an emotional journey because I love the Church. It is the Church that has carried me through the most triumphant and traumatic parts of my life. The Church introduced me to the love, compassion, and grace that can only be found in Jesus when I felt unloved, misunderstood, and condemned. However, over the past few years, the Lord has begun to show me the specs of dirt and the grittiness that exist within His Church. He has slowly opened my eyes to show me how pride, self-righteousness, selfishness, and judgment have caused divisiveness, resulting in blemishes in what He wants to be a spotless Bride. We were never meant to be divided, we were meant to be one. One with Jesus as He is one with the Father.

We are created for His purpose and His work to build His Kingdom here on Earth.

So, what does building the Kingdom look like? Spending a long time in church culture you begin to speak the language and use certain words. We have a vernacular that's common amongst all of us, but we don't always know exactly what those words mean. My hope is that by reading this book, just as Jesus was moved by compassion to heal and help the broken, you will also be moved to action. My prayer is your perspective will change and in doing so you will be activated to be the move of God in your community. You will learn about the underlying causes of problems in our society and how Jesus, through the local church, is the only answer to those problems. You'll also learn about how far the church has drifted from the original mission that Jesus spoke about. And lastly, I never want to leave you with all the things that you should do without telling you how to do them. The last part of this book will be focused on how your church can begin to have an impact on the local community and really love their neighbors. Jesus said to the apostles, "You will be my witnesses in Jerusalem, and in all Judea and Samaria, and to the ends of the Earth" (Acts 1:8, NIV). The heart behind this book is to help you and your church establish ministry in your Jerusalem.

At the end of each chapter, I will include scriptures and questions to help you reflect on the concepts discussed. This book is not intended to be read passively; it is a call to action for the individual and the collective church. I encourage you to work through the scriptures and questions provided to allow the Lord to deepen your understanding. Mobilizing the church to action is just as much about the personal journey you will experience as it is about seeing a corporate transformation.

Reflection

Read Psalm 139: 23-24

Take some time to ask the Lord, what biases might exist in you in regards to the poor or perhaps how the church operates about caring for the poor.

Read Matthew 25:31-46

What emotions come up when you read this passage? In what ways do you do what Jesus is talking about here? What about your church? What could get in the way of your church being mobilized to care for those in need?

Prayer

Father, help me to see people the way that you do. Stir in me the compassion that Jesus had when he saw those who were suffering. Search my heart and root out anything that would keep me from loving people the way that you love them. As I read this book, help me to connect with Jesus' heart for the lost and the needy. Help me to be a reflection of your goodness, kindness, love and mercy. In Jesus Name, Amen.

Chapter 2

"Charity is not a substitute for justice withheld."
— *St. Augustine*

A keynote speaker at a healthcare conference I attended spoke about how our address predicts our life expectancy. I had known this previously, but what really brought this fact to life was an illustration he used. He gave an example of a real city that had a subway and he calculated that if someone rode from point A to point D on that subway, that person would lose about 3 years of life for each mile the subway traveled toward point D. When I heard this, all I could think of was the scripture John 10:10, "The thief does not come except to steal, and to kill, and to destroy. I have come that they may have life, and that they may have *it* more abundantly" (NKJV). While I listened to him describe the impact of poverty on social determinants of health (which I will explain later) and poor health outcomes, I couldn't help but to be moved by the Holy Spirit as He revealed to me the issues underlying these problems and how the only answer to solving them is Jesus. There are nearly 38 million people in the United States living in poverty and they need our help. However, even in the Church, accusations made about people who are poor run rampant. My hope is that this chapter provides you with insight as to how complex poverty is and the factors that keep individuals living in poverty so that we, as a Church, can begin to bring the abundance of Jesus to our communities.

Recently a new phenomenon called deaths of despair has been discovered by researchers Ann Cates and Angus Deaton. Deaths of despair are deaths attributed to drug abuse, alcohol abuse, or suicide; although, they claim that all three are a form of suicide. These deaths of despair are impacting not the minorities, but middle-aged White men who do not have a college degree. The researcher showed that not only have these deaths been occurring at alarming rates, but over decades the rate has silently been rising with each generation. The cause for these deaths? Cumulative distress caused by the weakness of the family structure, overall sense of upheaval in the social environment, poor physical and mental health, emotional pain, difficulty socializing, difficulty relaxing, increased body mass index, not being married, not being attached to the workforce, and not being affiliated with a religion. In fact, these deaths are so prevalent that they are impacting the overall life expectancy rates for the United States causing a steady decrease over the last decade. And while the rates for deaths of despair are highest in men, women are also affected. Additionally, the mortality rates, or the measurement of deaths for a population during a given time, have worsened for the groups affected most by deaths of despair. For many years, Latinos and Blacks have had much higher mortality rates, but that gap is closing with the onset of deaths of despair. Poverty impacts all people of all genders and races. There is no single cause, but an accumulation of many causes that creates more and more oppression for the individuals and their families. The cause of poverty, according to research, includes lack of employment, debt, trauma, addiction, and the weakened state of the family unit. However, I believe that poverty is a spiritual issue at its root. It manifests in people's lives due to a lack of understanding about their identity in Jesus. Poverty thrives in our communities because people are living under a false belief system about what their life could be, and as a result they've lost their hope—plummeting themselves into despair.

A Life Built on Lies

Imagine an innocent baby just entering the world. This baby is joyful and full of hope for the future because he doesn't have to carry the burdens of today and every moment and thought is full of possibility. As children grow up, depending on their environment, they are taught limits and what to believe about themselves and the world. A child who lives in poverty must overcome challenges that many of us never have to face: lack of basic physical and emotional needs being met, living in a single parent home, caring for younger siblings or a parent who has mental illness or substance abuse, lack of stability in their home, and/or homelessness, to name a few. These are burdens that children are not equipped to process in a healthy way. If the light of hope within them isn't well tended, it begins to dim with the darkness of the world they face and the challenges ahead of them. The future, all of a sudden doesn't seem so hopeful and worry, anger, and resentment begin to replace where love, joy, and peace once were. Their living environments aren't safe so it increases their anxiety and depression, which sets down the roots for fear and ambivalence. The cycle of poverty continues as kids begin to attend school and their challenges at home make it difficult for them to perform well. They may lose interest in getting good grades and begin to think, "No one in my family has made anything of themselves. Why bother?" They may go on to think thoughts such as, "Why should I put time into doing school work? No one cares about me anyway. I'll probably never get out of this neighborhood." Kids who live in these environments look around to those who aren't struggling and begin to model their behavior. Unfortunately, those people may not be good role models. Perhaps now this baby is now a teenager and decides to join a gang because they see how the other gang members have money and treat each other like family. Now, they have the resources to live and the support system they didn't have when at home. As the child transitions to adulthood, they have been in and out of jail multiple times. Maybe by the time they reach their thirties, they decide to change their way of life and are ready to get a job, but their choices are limited because of their legal history, lack of education, skills, and work history. As the story goes on and on, we can see how things that are not within a child's control can have an immeasurable impact on how they grow up and those issues and beliefs can follow them to adulthood. And, this cycle repeats over and over from generation to generation.

What is more damaging, is throughout their life, they may have people telling them lies about what they deserve, what they are capable of, and how they should view their world thereby shaping their identity. The problem with those who have experienced trauma, poverty, and instability is that *the enemy* has stolen their identity. There are demonic influences that plant thoughts in their minds that negatively impact their impressions of themselves and God. These thoughts are lies they believe throughout their life if they don't have someone replacing these thoughts with the truth which is firmly rooted in the Word of God. The devil does this to keep them from knowing who God is and who they are created to be. The process of undoing these lies is what brings healing and freedom. Romans 12:2 says to "be transformed by the renewing of your mind" (NIV). And, just to make sure those seeds of deception grow, he uses people and government policies and systems to continue to oppress people who are living in poverty. The real travesty is that they don't realize this is what has happened to them. If we look at poverty as a case of stolen identity, we begin to see how the thoughts and systems work against an individual being able to have the opportunity to experience their true selves. It is only when they encounter the healing power of Jesus that they will experience true transformation.

There is much research available that shows the relationship between poverty and the trajectory of a person's life. While it isn't known which comes first, poverty or negative childhood experiences, the research supports that there is a definite relationship between the two. The way that we research and measure those negative childhood experiences is by obtaining adverse childhood experience (ACE) scores. There was a well-known study performed by the Centers for Disease Control and Prevention (CDC) and Kaiser Permanente in the late 1990s that looked at ACEs in a population of more than 1,700 individuals in California. ACEs are experiences that occur before the age of 18 that could be harmful or traumatic and have long-lasting effects on the individual's wellness. These experiences include things like abuse, neglect, and instability in the family dynamic. The purpose of the Kaiser Permanente study was to understand the long-term impact of these experiences.

The general framework of the study is represented by the diagram below. The study showed there is a strong relationship between ACEs and wellbeing. Children who grow up in poverty are at a much higher risk of having these adverse experiences. Children who have higher ACE scores are more likely to have lower performance in school and engage in risky behaviors such as alcohol and/or substance abuse and unprotected sex. In adulthood, people with high ACE scores are prone to poverty, mental health issues such as depression and anxiety, difficulty keeping a job, and/or being more likely to be incarcerated. Further, they are more likely to have chronic diseases like sexually transmitted infections, heart disease, diabetes, and cancer.

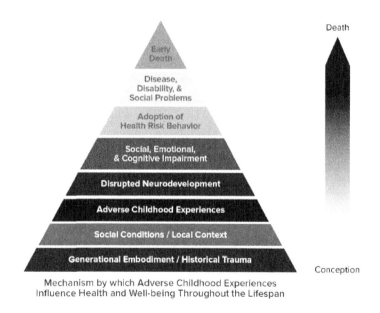

Mechanism by which Adverse Childhood Experiences
Influence Health and Well-being Throughout the Lifespan

Source: Centers for Disease Control and Prevention

14

Most likely when I described the newborn baby earlier you may have had some compassion because children should never have to face the hardships that many face growing up in poverty. The problem is, we lose compassion when that child reaches a certain age. We begin to blame them for their station in life and fail to recognize all the circumstances that lead them to that station in the first place. Back to the issue of identity and poverty, how can we expect someone who is living in poverty to have the capacity to improve their situation when, quite frankly, they don't believe that they can or that they even deserve to have a better life. Many of these people live without hope for a future of any kind. Can you fathom a life without hope? When I began working with people living in this hopeless state, it was difficult for me to wrap my brain around it. In fact, once I met with a young woman who had gotten into some trouble and had reached out to ask me for some gas money. She wasn't able to work because her babysitter had quit. During our conversation, I asked her, "When you think about your life and your goals, what do you see? What do you want to do with it?" When I finished asking the question, she stared at me blankly for a moment. She couldn't answer the question. In fact, I think I may have been the first person to ever ask her this question. As she scrambled to answer the question, I could tell that she hadn't thought of the prospect of a future. Or, if she had thought of it, it was only for a brief moment before the reality of her life set in. People who live in poverty are so busy trying to make things work for today that many don't have the emotional bandwidth to think about tomorrow.

How do these thoughts contrast with their true identity? Many children who grow up in unhealthy environments, which often accompany poverty, struggle with an orphan spirit. They believe they are unloved, rejected, worthless, and that there is no hope for their future. These beliefs have a major impact on their adult life. By adulthood, those beliefs are firmly rooted and will have blossomed into their identity; who they think they are which gives way to a poverty mindset. Poverty mindset is a set of beliefs that a person is a victim of their circumstance and that things like money, food, and shelter will always be a scarcity. It is the acceptance that this is life as they know it and it won't get any better because it is their cross to bear, so to speak. However, the catch is this belief system also gives a tarnished view of not only who they are, but who God the Father is. The enemy spins a lie that they are living the way they are because God is purposely oppressing people and withholding blessings or even punishing them. Whether the person consciously believes this representation of God or not, their view of God as a loving Father is negatively altered because of their childhood and current experiences. Additionally, this skewed view of money keeps poverty-stricken people in a bondage that they can't possibly free themselves from without the healing that comes from encountering who God is and the gift of love, grace, and redemption found in Christ.

There is a chart that helps me keep a pulse on my own identity in Christ, but also helps serve as a point of reference when working with people. The chart contrasts the difference between a person living with an orphan spirit and someone who lives within sonship. I encourage you to take some time to study this chart. Firstly, think about yourself. Are there areas where sonship hasn't fully been manifested? Secondly, think about someone you have worked with or encountered living in poverty. You can start to see how many of their behaviors are rooted in characteristics often seen in someone who struggles with an orphan spirit.

For example, the first item in the chart is related to their image of who God is. If they see God as a master (*orphan*) and not God as a loving father (*sonship*), they may believe that He doesn't care about their circumstances and that He is actually purposefully withholding His blessing or punishing them. A master is someone who uses a position of power or authority to rule over people for selfish gain. If this is how they view God, they won't want to connect with Him as a loving father who cares for His children and is generous. Further, if they believe they can rely only on themselves (orphan), they won't trust in God to provide (sonship) or even ask to give Him the opportunity to provide. Even worse, they may seek counterfeit affections (orphan) and fall into alcoholism, substance abuse, or risky sexual behaviors rather than seeking Him as the source of their comfort (sonship). Having an identity that is not aligned with sonship is not reserved for only those who are poor. However, those who grow up in poverty certainly are not at an advantage. We also know that these defeating attitudes and beliefs are more prominent in this population. With each belief attached to the orphan spirit, the farther away the individual is positioned from living life in abundance and having hope for the future.

	Living as an orphan	Living as son or daughter
Relationship with God	God is a master, conditional, distant	God is a loving father, unconditional, close
Dependence	Can only rely on self	Depends on God
Theology	Fear, rule-based	Lives by grace and love
Security	Insecure and lacks peace	Lives in rest and peace
Need for Approval	Seeks praise and acceptance	Knows accepted and loved by God
Motivation	Strives to prove themselves to others and God	Driven to serve by love for God and others
View of Self	Based on comparison to others	Based on identity in Christ
Source of Comfort	Addictions, compulsions, material possessions, busyness	Experiencing God's presence in prayer and solitude
Relationship with Others	Competitive, jealous of others	Humility, seeks the interests of others
Handling Faults in themselves and others	Accusatory, intentionally seeks to put down others, unaware of own faults or unwilling to address them	Self-reflective, asks God to restore faults, seeks to restore others
View of Authority	Sees authority as controlling, not to be trusted, unwilling to submit to authority of others	Honors and respects those in authority, see them as trustworthy and a source of wisdom
Correction or Criticism	Difficulty receiving correction or criticism, easily offended and hurt, blames others and unwilling to accept responsibility	Grateful for correction and recognizes it is necessary for growth
Giving and Receiving Love	Untrusting, loves conditionally usually based on others meeting expectations	Open, trusting, patient, self-sacrificial, and compassionate towards others
Position in Life	Slave, powerless, victim	Son/Daughter, powerful, victorious
View of the Future	Unable to see a future or view it in a positive way	Hopeful, full of possibilities

The Impact of Hope

Hope can have a profound effect on a person's life and future. We know that just the presence of hope can improve a cancer patient's quality of life. We also know that interventions of hope in inner-city school-aged kids improves their performance in school. In their article, "Poverty, Aspirations, and the Economics of Hope," authors Travis J. Lybbert and Bruce Wydick study the impact of hope in the poor.

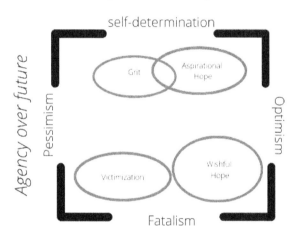

Perceptions about future

This diagram illustrates a few things: a person's ability to impact their future (agency) and their beliefs about the future itself (negative or positive). As an example, if someone has a low agency to impact their future and a negative view of the future, this person might behave and think like a victim, which Lybbert and Wydick say, "is a particularly desperate form of hopelessness, as it is accompanied by perceived helplessness." Conversely, if someone has a high agency to impact their future and a positive perception, this will bring about aspirational hope. It is through the intersection of both skills and hope that someone can begin to shift from just being hopeful to actually achieving their dreams. Without hope, one could not aspire to develop more skills or make plans. The conclusion of their research showed that the presence of hope as an intrinsic motivator paired with skills can help individuals transition out of poverty.

Poverty and Health

The World Health Organization (WHO) describes social determinants of health (SDOH) as the conditions in which people are born, grow, work, live and age, and the wider set of forces and systems that shape the conditions of daily life. SDOH are important because in a time when our country is literally experiencing a healthcare crisis, it is these determinants which summarize barriers that people may experience in having the opportunity to have health (or life in abundance). For those who have not experienced poverty, not having the opportunity for health (not just access to health care services) may seem like an exaggeration. The WHO defines health as "a state of complete physical, mental and social well-being and not merely the absence of disease or infirmity." When a person experiences these barriers, it can put them at a higher risk for poor health outcomes or impede their ability to seek care when they are ill, but these barriers also take away access to things like healthy foods or outdoor spaces to ride a bike or walk. In turn, this takes away their ability to be healthy in the first place. I think it is important to note that even the WHO recognizes the need for wholeness in all aspects of a persons' life. This is the very thing that Jesus came to bring to the world. It is interesting that the world recognizes the need and is attempting to meet it. What needs to happen, however, is the Church needs to be at the forefront meeting these practical needs, but sharing the Gospel which is the answer to the intrinsic and extrinsic contributing factors for poverty. If hope has the power to transition someone from poverty, then is it far-fetched to connect that The Hope of the world is the answer? The social determinants of health include six categories: Neighborhood and Built Environments, Economic Stability, Education and Early Childhood Education and Development, Social and Community Context, and Health and Healthcare. As I review each of these categories, I think you will find that the impact is actually farther reaching than just healthcare, but that not having these things in place actually diminishes their chance at health. It is important to understand that poverty is a much bigger problem than an individual or family not having enough money.

Neighborhood and Built Environments

The environment where a person lives is incredibly important. This includes the integrity of the home or shelter a person lives in or the neighborhood in which a person resides. There is a growing body of research called epigenetics that is showing that the environment, not just genetics, determines chronic illness in an individual. They are proving that the epigenetic markers for genes are responsible for turning on or off the genetic expression for certain diseases. These markers are influenced by the environment. For example, if a person that has a genetic predisposition for heart disease lives in a neighborhood that is unsafe and has no access to healthy food, these two factors can trigger the epigenetic marker to turn on the gene for heart disease. The unsafe neighborhood creates chronic stress from the fear they experience living in a neighborhood with a high violent crime rate. Or, the lack of safety prevents them from walking outside, taking their children to public parks, or lacking access to a public park in their neighborhood. Maybe they live in an area where there is only a convenience store and there is no public transportation to get them to a grocery store to access healthy, fresh foods. If that same person lives in a safe environment and has access to the food they need to be healthy, that epigenetic marker may not turn on the genetic expression of heart disease. All of these things play an integral role in someone's health, but are mostly out of the person's control because they are structural elements within communities.

Economic Stability

Money is what we think of most often when we think of the poor because the very word poverty is associated with not having enough of it. But, the impact of not having economic stability has many implications beyond not having enough money. For example, if someone has the means to afford transportation to get to and from work, they may be unable to pay for gas or insurance. Thus, not having adequate transportation could limit their options for gainful employment. But, there are also barriers that get in the way of getting employment. For example, most employers require at least a high school diploma or GED to be hired. However, there are many jobs that someone who does not have a high school diploma or GED could do. Or, perhaps someone who has previously been incarcerated for a non-violent crime, they may not be hired because of their past. As with most of the social determinants of health, there are structural challenges related to wages and cost of living. Someone working 40 hours a week, making $12/hour, would bring home around $1300 a month. This person could get an apartment (depending on where they lived) for around $650/month. That leaves them with only $700 to pay for food, phone, utilities, and if they have a vehicle, gas and insurance. The problem is that low cost rentals are few and far between. Most cities are developing luxury housing to attract a more affluent population. Therefore, a more realistic scenario would be that this person would get an apartment or mobile home paying $800/month, cutting the funds for other expenses to $500 a month. Additionally, the stress of not having enough to cover living expenses can also trigger epigenetic markers, access to healthy food, and the location where they live. Further, the stress of having less than what is needed can cause chronic stress which can lead to physical and mental illness and even impede brain development in children.

Education

Lack of education is the most impactful contributing cause for poverty. But, in turn, poverty is a major contributing factor to the lack of education. It makes sense that the more education a person has (traditional or vocational), the more money a person will make. Therefore, it stands to reason the less opportunity you have for education negatively impacts the amount of money a person could make. There are many reasons that children and adults do not have access to education, but most of them are rooted in having the financial means to live in a good school district or to afford higher education. And, the effect of not having education is that the cycle of poverty continues to the next generation.

You may be noticing that these determinants do not each live in a vacuum. Most often, there is a cascade that occurs when just one of the determinants is in a cautionary position. If an individual does not get a solid education or they do not pursue vocational or higher education in adulthood, this impacts their ability to obtain viable employment. Literacy and social competencies can also be affected when there is a lack of education. For example, a person who has Type 2 diabetes who is living in poverty is at risk for inefficiencies in processing sugar because of the increased stress hormones being produced within the body. Additionally, this person may be living in a food desert, a geographical location where fresh fruits and vegetables are not available. These are only two barriers to health that a person living in poverty might face and neither are within their control. Hypothetically, even if someone living in poverty is able to get medical care, their literacy level is likely to be low. Many may not understand how to manage their own care of that chronic disease.

Social and Community Context
Having a social and community context refers to the setting or circumstances that the person or persons are living in. This could mean the neighborhood or city they live in or what religious or social organizations they belong to and how engaged they are in those organizations. Does the person have healthy relationships? A support system? What is their culture within their neighborhood or community? Do they belong to a population related to race, gender, or sexual preference that experiences discrimination? What are the societal and community factors that might negatively impact their well-being? Further, social context can have an overall effect on the person and their emotional well-being. As mentioned in this chapter, hope and agency impact an individual's future. If their social context reinforces behaviors, beliefs, and ideas about the future, it makes sense that the person will believe those things.

Health and Healthcare
When someone is unable to get access to health care, it causes a domino effect. The first, and most obvious impact, is that they don't

get better. Having untreated illness can also contribute to poverty because the individual may not be able to go to work because of their illness. Additionally, children may miss school, which, as we explored earlier, has a lasting impact on their development and future. Healthcare is also expensive. People who struggle with poverty do not have the means to cover expensive premiums, which leads to being uninsured or underinsured. If they do have insurance coverage, it is more often than not a plan that has a high deductible. Going to the doctor or hospital would mean high out of pocket cost and potentially debt. Lastly, if they do go to the doctor but don't have a job that offers paid time off, they will lose income.

While social determinants are used to understand why disparities in healthcare exist, they also help explain some of the challenges faced by those living in poverty. In fact, if we take a look at this diagram, we can see that 80% of a person's health is influenced by their physical environment, social and economic factors, and their health behaviors.

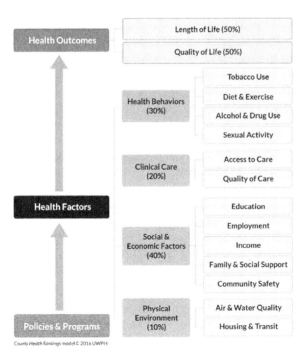

County Health Rankings model © 2016 UWPHI

23

Role of Debt in Poverty

Debt is a contributing factor to not only to poverty, but also keeping people living in poverty. There is a cycle that occurs in the lives of those living in poverty. There is a cliché used to describe it that goes like this, "You have to borrow from Peter to pay Paul." What happens in the lives of those living in this position is that they are constantly reshuffling their resources in order to address the most urgent of needs. In some months, they might miss paying the telephone bill to keep the heat on. However, what happens is that they just owe double next month. So, the next month, they pay down their bills and then they are short on rent. It is an endless cycle of lack. Eventually, all these instances of borrowing add up. Utilities are turned off and so then they take from the rent, which leads to being behind and then eventually turns into an eviction. Once a family has an eviction on their record, they are negatively impacted in many ways. They are unable to get low-income housing until they pay back the money owed from the eviction. Their options are greatly decreased and most often they end up either homeless or signing to get housing that they are unable to afford to keep their family from being homeless.

Signing a lease for housing they can't afford may not sound wise to most of us. We would chalk this up to bad decision making. However, to someone living in poverty, their goal is to take care of the crisis today and worry about tomorrow's crisis tomorrow. Keeping a roof over their family's head was the priority and they achieved that. However, it enters them back into the cycle of lack and debt. This is why assisting people with emergency needs is so critical. If we help manage the crisis, they can refocus the little resources they have on the future.

There is a lot of complexity when we think about poverty and social determinants of health. And, certainly, not every issue can be given the justice it deserves in just this one chapter and we didn't touch on the issue of disparity, or reasons why one group of people experiences challenges or barriers more than others. However, what

I hope you get from this chapter is that poverty is so much more than not having enough money or working harder. People who are in poverty are just victims of their circumstances who despite their best efforts have the cards stacked against them. Those cards keep them in poverty and reinforce negative thoughts about what is possible or what they are capable of. They, in essence, are just the adult version of an innocent child who has been set up against difficult and sometimes horrific circumstances that cycles repeatedly from generation to generation. Poverty is not a life that a person willfully chooses, but is a form of bondage of the mind that imprisons those it has captured into a hole that they can't possibly climb out of by themselves. Poverty is a physical manifestation of a very real, deep rooted spiritual problem caused by circumstances that were out of their control, which has led them to debilitating belief systems and not fully knowing their identity in Christ.

Reflection

Read John 10:10
What does having life in abundance mean to you? What do you think Jesus meant when He said that?

Read Luke 4:18-19
Why do you think Jesus said that He was to bring good news to the poor? Why do you think the poor matter so much to God?

Prayer

Father, help me to love those who need love the most. Open my eyes to see things the way that you do. Help me to look past what is known on the surface about those living in poverty and connect with the deeper issues that cause this oppression. Teach me what it means to live life in abundance so that I can help others to do so. In Jesus Name, Amen.

Chapter 3

Let us not make a mistake that the hunger is only for a piece of bread. The hunger today is so much greater: the hunger for love, to be wanted, to be loved, to be cared for, to be somebody.

—Mother Teresa

Whatever the causes of poverty, the bottom line is that God cares about the poor. And, because He cares about the poor, we should. All throughout Scripture, God cautions us to not overlook these people. God says He "loves justice" in Isaiah 61:8. Justice, to the secular person, might translate to passing judgement to give people what they have coming to them. In essence, if you commit a crime, you pay the time. When this happens, we feel like justice has been done. Isn't this the way we sometimes think about people who are in poverty? That their poverty is in fact just because of their own decisions and actions? Biblical justice isn't what we interpret it to mean, however. We view justice through our own perspective and experiences, which often leads to an interpretation that God longs to punish us and throw us into the pit of Hell because of our transgressions. If that were the case, why would David write, "Judge me, O Lord, according to my righteousness" (Psalm 7:8, ESV)? David was asking God to evaluate his actions and be honest about what they reflect. He was pleading to God to honestly tell him if he measured up to God's standard of righteousness? And, if not, restore him so that he could be made new again. That is what biblical justice or God's judgment is about.

It is God's evaluation of our behavior and His working to bring restoration to that area of our life.

What is God referring to when He says that He loves justice? God's version of justice is that we should treat every person with value or as if they are the image of God (Genesis 1:27). In Micah 6:8, the Prophet's message from God says, "He has shown you, O mortal, what is good. And what does the Lord require of you? To act justly and to love mercy and to walk humbly with your God" (NIV). God requires us to be actively engaged in practicing justice and bringing justice to our world by being an advocate or working to change the social structures that oppress people. Scripture says in Proverbs 31:8-9, "Speak up for those who cannot speak for themselves, for the rights of all who are destitute. Speak up and judge fairly; defend the rights of the poor and needy" (NIV). How can this happen if we are not purposeful in helping those in need? Having mercy on those who need it? How can we say we walk with God and obey Him, but do not take into consideration His clear instructions to do these things? God says through the Prophet Jeremiah very clearly, "This is what the Lord says: Do what is just and right. Rescue from the hand of the oppressor, the one who has been robbed. Do no wrong or violence to the foreigner, the fatherless or the widow." God is calling us to live in a radically selfless manner. Over and over, God tells us to not overlook those in poverty, but to actively work to help them.

Poverty has a compounding effect on a person's well-being and health. But, what is our response to someone who lives in this dire state? It is not uncommon that many biases surface. Most of the time when I speak to people about the work I do with those living in poverty, people tend to make a couple of assumptions. First, they tell me that people who live in that situation want to be there and that they choose to allow themselves to remain in that situation. Second, they tell me that people who are poor, live that way because they don't manage their money and so we shouldn't give to them because it is their own fault they don't have enough. Or, we shouldn't give to people because they are just going to spend it on cigarettes, alcohol, or drugs. Well, at least, these are the assumptions people are most likely to admit. There are also personal biases at play based on judgements having to do with gender, race, sexual orientation, and mental health. The judgements, which are almost immediate, are called implicit biases. Every person has implicit bias because we filter our impressions on someone based on our own experiences and feelings. When I share with people, inside and outside of the church, what I do for ministry and talk about how we are working in a community or neighborhood, I am met with some sort of criticism based on their individual opinions about why "those people" are in that situation. However, when I hear this from believers, it saddens me just a bit more. When we form an opinion about people who live in poverty, we are condemning them for the sins of the past that may or may not belong to them. When I think of this, my thoughts always turn to the story of Mary Magdalene. The religious leaders had dragged her out and surrounded her to condemn her to death for her sins. But, Jesus stepped between the judged, Mary Magdalene, to protect her. He knew everything she had done and would do and He didn't condemn her. Instead, He chose to love her by showing mercy. I also speculate that Jesus knew the circumstances that Mary faced and why she ended up living a life a prostitution. It could have been because she was forced to do so. Maybe she was sold by her family. Or, maybe she had no family and the only option for a single woman during that time in history was to make a living through prostitution. Jesus saw past the circumstance and saw the person and exercised mercy. I think it is also important to note that Mary's decisions could have been the result of a system that she belonged to but had no control over. This is the same for those who live in poverty, as well. Many who live in poverty are in situations where they are forced to make decisions that go against their values for the sake of surviving for that day.

James 2:12-13 warns us to, "Speak and act [consistently] as people who are going to be judged by the law of liberty [that moral law that frees obedient Christians from the bondage of sin]. For judgment will be merciless to one who has shown no mercy; but [to the one who has shown mercy] mercy triumphs [victoriously] over judgment" (AMP). The Apostle James is telling us that God favors mercy above doing all the right things a Christian should do. Many in the Church practice the opposite because they believe that it is their responsibility to point out the sins in others. Sometimes this leads to withholding assistance from those who might need it. But mercy, on the other hand, is about being compassionate even though it is in your power to discipline or punish. Mercy is not only withholding judgement, but exonerating the person. This is what Jesus did for us on the cross. He showed mercy to mankind even though we are rebellious and sinful. He pardoned us of our crimes where His blood covered us with grace.

Assumptions About People in Poverty

It is important to pause to address some of the assumptions that are made about people who live in poverty. As I mentioned, in discussions with people about helping the poor, I find some commonality exists within the rhetoric around helping the needy. If we are going to live a radical life centered on Christ like love, we need to be honest and evaluate those assumptions. These assumptions are believed to be the rule when dealing with poverty. However, the situations in which these assumptions may be true are actually the exception. I hope the following stories will demonstrate this.

ASSUMPTION #1: If they would just manage their money better or work harder, they could improve their situation

Jessa's Story: Jessa is a single mom who has three children under the age 8. She worked full time at a skilled nursing facility as a nurse's aide making $12/hour. She even picked up extra shifts when she could and had a babysitter for the children. Jessa had worked hard at her job and had demonstrated to her manager that she was ready to become a supervisor. Her manager was working to support her in this goal, and despite her lack of transportation, Jessa found a way to get to work every day.

However, regardless of how hard she worked, Jessa was wrongfully evicted from her low-income apartment and was now homeless. Jessa had been hurt on the job, which resulted in back surgery. Her doctor told her she needed to get an apartment on the ground level. When she asked her landlord to move her to a ground-level apartment, the landlord said that she had lied about her income and she had to pay $2,000 in order to stay living in her current apartment. While she was still able to get free legal aid to address the wrongful eviction, she found herself in a situation where she had an eviction on her record and needed a home in a hurry. By the time Jessa and I got connected, she had been living in a hotel for 3 weeks. While the hotel had an extremely low nightly rate, her entire paycheck and then some went to pay for this.

Typically, I try to help people navigate the existing resources available so that I can utilize the church resources for filling in the gap. So, my first step was to refer her to a local community action group that provides emergency rental support. However, in order for her to receive help, she had to either be in a shelter or in a hotel paid for by a non-profit or she wasn't considered literally homeless, and would therefore not be eligible to receive assistance. So, using church benevolence funds, I paid for Jessa and her children to stay in a hotel for a week hoping that she would get the rental assistance. She had an appointment with the local community action agency 5 days from when we contacted them. They asked her to begin looking for apartments. She wasn't able to find an apartment because she had an eviction on her record. Even though she was wrongfully evicted, any low-income housing had her blacklisted. So, we looked at the Section 8 waiting list in our area and found the list had been closed for 6 months. She wouldn't be able to move into low-income housing until she paid the debt from the eviction, which was around $2,000. But, she did find a trailer and had been approved for moving in once she had the money from the agency.

Five days came to pass and Jessa showed up for her appointment at the community action agency. The agency representative calculated her income for the last 30 days, only to find out that she made too much money from the overtime her boss had let her work over the last month (because she knew Jessa's situation), making her ineligible to receive assistance. Further, the money that they provide towards rental assistance cannot be used towards renting a trailer due to how the grant and policies are written. So Jessa, who receives a $300 paycheck each week, was living in a hotel which costs $330 a week. With a $30 deficit for just housing, how was she to pay for food, diapers, and other daily needs? For those who think all the poor need is a good money management system, the question becomes: How do people in poverty manage money they simply don't have?

My next course of action was to then help her find a better paying job. However, when I asked Jessa if she wanted to work on that, she declined. At first, I admit, I was a little irritated by her response. However, after talking with her, I realized that she didn't want to leave because she had a boss who was supportive of her and her situation. She also had coworkers who helped her to get to work when she didn't have a ride. She didn't want to give up her existing support system at work until she felt more stable and she was holding out for that promotion to supervisor. I couldn't blame her for not wanting to obtain new employment after I understood why she felt that way. Her housing and daily needs were stressful and chaotic enough without upsetting the apple cart even more by starting a new job, as well as the unknown of whether they would be understanding of her situation. I continue to check in with Jessa and am currently trying to get her into a homeless shelter. We have two shelters in our area and both were full when I attempted to contact them. She is apprehensive about taking her children to a shelter. Who wouldn't be? But, this is the only way she will be able to save up money to pay her debt and save up enough to get a new place.

ASSUMPTION #2: People choose to be poor

Aubrey's Story: Aubrey is a single mom of two boys ages 10 and 12. She recently moved into a trailer after she and her husband divorced. Before this, she had been living in a middle-class neighborhood and was working as a stay-at-home mom. However, her husband had met someone new and filed for divorce. Once the divorce was final, she was forced into a situation where she had to find housing and a job to support herself and her two boys. She thought about moving in with her family who lived only 20 minutes away, but due to the constraints of their custody agreement, she wasn't allowed to move out of state and her family lived just over the Michigan border in Ohio. She found a mobile home park that had a promotion where she paid a deposit and first month's rent and then she got a month's free rent for signing. She had enough money to move into one of the trailers and signed the lease for $800/month. Through the negotiations of her divorce, she had been awarded child support. She figured she had the child support and she would be able to find something in the next couple of months to bring in some income to pay the rent. However, it wasn't until the third month that she was able to find a job in a plastics factory making $10/hour. She saved every penny she had, but since she had only worked a couple weeks in that third month, she fell short in paying that month's rent.

While the park management was willing to work with Aubrey to give her time to pay the rent before starting the eviction process for missing a month's rent, the agreement stated that fees would be accrued for late payments that were charged at first weekly and then daily rates. Aubrey attempted to pay off the previous month, but then the next month came and she was short from paying off the previous month's late fees and rent. She also had court fees because her ex-husband continued to call her into court to fight the custody agreement. So, she was behind another month in rent, but the management team worked with her again. By the time I met Aubrey, she was nearly 3 months behind, which was more than $3,000. She called our church after she had been declined rental support because she lived in a trailer. I wasn't able to raise enough money to keep her in her trailer, but was able to find her an apartment that was less money per month. Luckily, the landlord was her son's little league coach and he was willing to take a chance on her despite the eviction on her record.

A question I was asked by my church board was, "Why did she wait 3 months before asking for help?" The answer to that question is dignity. People who are in these types of situations genuinely believe that they will make it out. They don't want to have to ask for help. Aubrey had never been in a situation where her needs were not being met financially. She didn't choose to find herself in the situation that she was in. She was experiencing poverty because of decisions her husband had made.

While these are just two stories, these are the stories that are the norm and not the exception. Systems and policies are not built to help people out of poverty; they are built to keep them in. However, what is encouraging is that if we can help one person out of poverty, it will break the cycle of poverty for that family for the next generation.

Assumption #3: If they have money to buy cigarettes, they can pay for rent.

Once I explain to people the reasons why people live in poverty, I usually hear remarks such as, "Well, if they don't have money then how do they have money to buy cigarettes and alcohol?" or, "Don't give them cash, they will just spend it on booze or drugs." Interestingly, however, when you address poverty, substance abuse actually decreases. Instead of focusing on the vices these people may have, we need to understand these vices are often simply coping mechanisms for the underlying issues that are desperately in need of healing. But, in these situations, you obviously can't ignore if someone is an alcoholic or a drug addict. There is still wisdom and God gives it generously to those who ask (James 1:5). If there is a known substance abuse problem, those situations need to be handled differently. My approach for anyone I help is to not give the money directly to that person, but instead directly to the person or company needing to be paid. Additionally, I take advantage of the fact that they are asking for help to develop a relationship with them so that I can talk to them and get them help for substance abuse.

Assumption #4: It is not the Church's responsibility

Maybe it is hard to believe that this assumption exists in the church, but it does. Some churches are content to have a bus ministry or vacation bible school, but never actually help the families with practical needs. The overall sentiment is that it is simply our responsibility to share the Gospel. But, how can we share the Gospel without demonstrating it? There are many scriptures pointing us to helping those who are in need. Consider James 2:14-17 (NIV), "What good is it, my brothers and sisters, if someone claims to have faith but has no deeds? Can such faith save them? Suppose a brother or a sister is without clothes and daily food. If one of you says to them, 'Go in peace; keep warm and well fed,' but does nothing about their physical needs, what good is it? In the same way, faith by itself, if it is not accompanied by action, is dead."

Here are more Scriptures:
"It is a sin to despise one's neighbor, but blessed is the one who is kind to the needy." Proverbs 14:21 (NIV)

"Whoever oppresses the poor shows contempt for their Maker, but whoever is kind to the needy honors God." Proverbs 14:31 (NIV)

"I know that the Lord secures justice for the poor and upholds the cause of the needy." Psalm 140:12 (NIV)

"'For I was hungry and you gave me something to eat, I was thirsty and you gave me something to drink, I was a stranger and you invited me in, I needed clothes and you clothed me, I was sick and you looked after me, I was in prison and you came to visit me.' Then the righteous will answer him, 'Lord, when did we see you hungry and feed you, or thirsty and give you something to drink? When did we see you a stranger and invite you in, or needing clothes and clothe you? When did we see you sick or in prison and go to visit you?' The King will reply, 'Truly I tell you, whatever you did for one of the least of these brothers and sisters of mine, you did for me."" Matthew 25:35-40 (NIV)

While there are many more scriptures on this topic, I think it is safe to say it is very much the responsibility of the Church and the church organization to care for the poor. Some may say that this is the role of the individual Christian, but I disagree. The church organization absolutely has a responsibility for providing mechanisms and resources for this to happen. The church organization is the steward of the resources that have been given to them and should look to Scripture to understand what that looks like. Scripture says that money should be used in several ways: To care for those who preach God's Word and caring for the needy. However, this care for the needy in their local community is often an afterthought. Common practice is to forgo meeting needs in the local community and to use the money set aside in order to write checks that support worldwide missions. A less common practice in the church organization is to set aside a portion of the budget to address the needs in their local community through local organizations. An even less likely practice is using resources to get involved in what the needs of the community are and doing the work ourselves. But, here is what 1 John 3:17-19 says, "If a person owns the kinds of things we need to make it in the world but refuses to share with those in need, is it even possible that God's love lives in him? My little children, don't just talk about love as an idea or a theory. Make it your true way of life, and live in the pattern of gracious love" (Voice).

How can we say that we love God and that we are His Church, but neglect the thing that Jesus himself commanded us to do, which is to love people (Matthew 22:36-40)? Poverty and the symptoms of poverty can be overcome by supporting individuals and families within the community. This can be achieved by walking alongside those living in poverty by offering social and emotional support, which is the core of our church community. If our mission is to love God, love people, and make disciples, we should love God by loving what He loves. God cares deeply for those living in poverty, and we are called to express His love to others by being radically generous and doing practical acts of service. Some may make the argument that loving our neighbor is for the individuals within the Body of Christ, but the church organization is not held to a lower standard than the people of the church. In fact, the organization should be held to a higher standard because it has been entrusted with the resources the people have brought.

Assumption #5- If they want help, they should be coming to church.

Another behavior I have encountered is the notion that if we give to someone, they owe us something in return. It may not be an overt request for payment, but there is an unspoken expectation that we place on people when we help them. On some level, this is just human nature. If I donated a liver to someone, I would expect that they would no longer drink alcohol. We would think that something like that would be a gift. We see the ads all the time: "Give the gift of life." Inherently, the definition of a gift is giving something to someone without payment in return. However, how often do we give to others but attach an expectation onto what is supposed to be a gift? If we give to someone in need, do we expect them to come to church? Or, do we control how we give financial support, for example, by only giving food cards? I think there is an expectation that we put on people when we help them. We impose on them a new oppression of expectation. This is why we willingly give gifts of food, but are hesitant to give them cash or pay for housing costs. Somehow we think that food is a reasonable need above all the others and so we control what type of help we are willing to give. Instead, we should be asking in what ways do they need our help. I use money as the frame of reference for many of the mindsets and assumptions because money is what people seem to have the hardest time parting with. Most people would not argue that helping someone in poverty with job coaching or an education is reasonable. However, they might find it more difficult to accept paying for a $500 utility bill. It is usually the latter situation where the discussion changes and many questions ensue. We have certain expectations for how people should behave, and based on whether or not they meet our criteria we deem the person worthy or unworthy of receiving help, but this is not congruent with Scripture, "If, however, you are [really] fulfilling the Royal Law according to the Scripture, 'You shall love your neighbor as yourself [that is, if you have an unselfish concern for others and do things for their benefit]' you are doing well. But if you show partiality [prejudice, favoritism], you are committing sin and are convicted by the Law as offenders. For whoever keeps the whole Law but stumbles in one point, he has become guilty of [breaking] all of it" (James 2:8-10, AMP).

The Wrong Approach

There is an underlying desire people have when wanting to help others. It is this desire to see an immediate change or that their efforts have brought a positive impact. There is also this sense of responsibility. When we work with people, we tend to think that it is our job to make something happen. In actuality, it is only God who can change hearts. When we encounter someone who is in need, we expect them to have the desire to be better and to create a better life for themselves. It is confusing to us when someone isn't ready to jump in on finding a better job or getting job training. Let's think about Maslow's hierarchy of needs. Personal growth needs (getting a better job, building a better life) aren't present until the Cognitive level of the pyramid. There are many levels of needs that must be met before a person can get to the level where they are looking to grow and develop themselves.

However, when working with people in poverty, how often do we expect that people should just want to be a better version of themselves (self-actualization)? We skip over all the other needs they might have and jump right to the top.

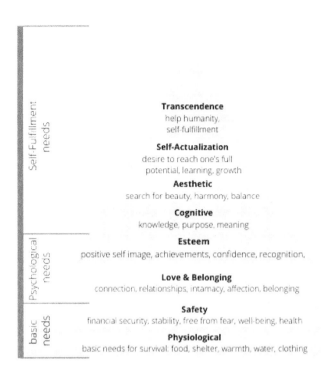

Transcendence
help humanity,
self-fulfillment

Self-Actualization
desire to reach one's full
potential, learning, growth

Aesthetic
search for beauty, harmony, balance

Cognitive
knowledge, purpose, meaning

Esteem
positive self image, achievements, confidence, recognition,

Love & Belonging
connection, relationships, intamacy, affection, belonging

Safety
financial security, stability, free from fear, well-being, health

Physiological
basic needs for survival: food, shelter, warmth, water, clothing

If someone doesn't have food, shelter, or water, how can we expect them to be ready for self-improvement? It is ludicrous to think that they are ready to embark on such an endeavor. Yet, this is often what happens to those who are underprivileged. Basic physiological needs must be met before a person can move up the hierarchy of needs. Working with those living in poverty is a long game. It isn't a simple sermon, mic drop, and it is all done. It can be a slow process built on relationships and community with those you serve. You are building trust so that they can feel safe in forming a lasting relationship. It will be difficult for anyone to maintain healthy relationships if they are constantly looking to meet physiological and safety needs. Maslow did clarify that not all needs have to be met to move up the hierarchy and there may be some back and forth within the levels. Having most of the needs satisfied can motivate a person to begin working up the hierarchy. Perhaps once their physical and safety needs are met, a person may be mentally and emotionally ready to think about friendships and family relationships. It is through healthy relationships that people begin to develop positive self-perception and responsibility to others. In the last chapter we discussed this from a belief mindset perspective. It isn't until this point that the beliefs about their identity and capabilities can begin to be addressed and transformed. All the levels up to this point are considered what Maslow called "deficiency needs." These needs arise because they are lacking in basic needs.

Maslow's theory states that the deficiencies themselves will motivate people to have them met. For example, the hungrier someone gets, the more they will be motivated to find food. However, motivation isn't enough if you are living in poverty because motivation does not equal accessibility. Instead of focusing on meeting their needs, people in poverty are fighting to work through a system that is inefficient and challenging to navigate. At every step of the process there is screening and paperwork and requirements that must be satisfied to move forward. And, all the components of the system don't talk to each other. It is a pipe that has a clog every few feet that has offshoots that may not lead back to the main pipeline when needed. People get lost, they get frustrated. Additionally, there is a tipping point of when the system spits them out. If a person does make progress and they begin to make a little more, the system says, "You don't need us anymore," and strips away the help they may have still been needing.

There is a woman I had been helping for a while who had held down a job as a retail clerk. She was working full time and received a raise from $10/hour to $10.60/hour. Before taxes, that is just shy of $1,700 a month. Now, factor in taxes, rent, phone, and utilities: there isn't much left. Getting that 60 cent raise, however, cut her food stamps by 25%. Did getting this raise really get her further away from poverty or did it make it worse? She was already finding it difficult to pay for her bills and other needs. That extra money could have helped alleviate financial distress or used to pay off bills or save for a car, but instead it is now reallocated to covering the cost of food which was previously covered through receiving assistance.

Eventually, we do need to help people to transition to what Maslow refers to as self-fulfillment needs. The way the Church can help people is through discipleship and relationship with God. Without discipleship, a person may never move up the pyramid to "self-esteem." This is where people begin to discover their identity. Which, as we discussed in the last chapter, is the foundation for changing mindsets and behaviors. I had grown up in the church and hadn't really understood this concept of identity until I was well into adulthood. This is why so many Christians, not just those who live in poverty, continue to live in their brokenness. We stopped at "belonging" and didn't help people discover who God created them to be. If they don't understand this, if one doesn't really get who they are, they won't be able to progress to living a life of fullness in Christ. As disciple-makers, it is our commission to help people learn this.

The Enemy knows this and is actively working to press people further into the lower levels of this hierarchy. Because the further down he can push people the more discouragement, resentment, and anger they feel. At every layer he creates chaos, confusion, and division amongst people. He plants lies about God and about His Church. We must help people discover the lies they believe about themselves. We have to be attentive to how the enemy is working and the tactics he employs to bring oppression and bondage into this world. We can no longer continue to do Church "as usual." If we want to pray, "on Earth as it is in Heaven," then, we must be ready to get to work by helping people through this process and potentially assisting them with meeting basic needs until they get there.

As such, our approach must change. Reaching non-believers, in the Western Church, for the most part consists of hosting events and drawing on numbers of people. I heard it once said that the health of a church is counted in "nickels and noses." This approach translates to traditional outreach initiatives. If we get a lot of people at an event, it is successful. However, how many people are actually changed by these large-scale events? It is almost as if we think that because we host a fun event and people get to hang out with us, that our Jesus dust will rub off on them and magically they will accept Jesus as their savior. Would we be willing to consider that maybe approaching reaching unbelievers in this way is using the wrong approach? Real transformation happens when someone is able to encounter Jesus and through a meaningful connection with one of His people.

Balint, T., Pangaro, P. (2017, September). Maslow's Hierarchy of Needs [Digital image]. Retrieved August 20, 2020, from https://www.researchgate. net/figure/Maslows-Hierarchy-of-Needs-HoN-mapped-into-astronaut-needs-and-risk-mitigation_fig2_320224483

Reflection

Read 1 John 3:17-19

How does this verse challenge you personally? How do you think this verse contrasts or supports how your church operates today?

Take some time to reflect on what biases you have about people who are poor. Write them down. Next, ask God to reveal to you how He views the poor. Write His response in a journal.

Prayer

Holy Spirit, reveal to me anything that is in my heart related to mindsets or assumptions towards those who live in poverty. Replace my thoughts with your thoughts. Speak to me about your heart for them. Break my heart for the things that break your heart. In Jesus Name, Amen.

Chapter 4

*"He naturalizes Divine Love as a fully human expression.
This is how He wants us to 'be with' each other and particularly
the broken and hurting among us."*
—J.D. Walt

One misconception that exists within the Church is that the work of outreach or caring for the poor are for the few and not the masses, but this assumption is incorrect. Our current approach for outreach and caring for the poor is typically one of the following: plan a big event, volunteer a weekend, and/or send a check to a non-profit, mission, or evangelical ministry. Money and time is a great way to support these efforts at an individual level, but not so for a church organization. The church organization should be mobilizing and organizing ways for their church members to learn how to be the move of God in their communities every day.

According to Scripture, however, every person is responsible for caring for others. In Matthew 22:37-40, Jesus was asked what the greatest commandment is and He responded, "'Love the Lord your God with all your heart and with all your soul and with all your mind.' This is the first and greatest commandment. And the second is like it: 'Love your neighbor as yourself.' All the Law and the Prophets hang on these two commandments" (NIV). The word *neighbor* doesn't mean just those who live within your circle of influence. In fact, the word is more accurately translated to "all of mankind." Scripture also says in 1 John 4:10-12, 19-21, "This is love: not that we loved God, but that He loved us and sent His Son as an atoning sacrifice for our sins. Dear friends, since God so loved us, we also ought to love one another. No one has ever seen God; but if we love one another, God lives in us and His love is made complete in us … We love because He first loved us. Whoever claims to love God yet hates a brother or sister is a liar. For whoever does not love their brother and sister, whom they have seen, cannot love God whom they have not seen. And He has given us this command: Anyone who loves God must also love their brother and sister" (NIV). Loving others is not only the outward expression of God 's love for us, but it is also the mechanism in which we remain in His love.

The first question we must ask is what is love? There are many different kinds of love. There is parental love, romantic love, and the relational love we have for friends and families. We even use the word love to describe how we feel about inanimate objects. However, the New Testament has three Greek words that are used to refer to love in the Bible. The first type of love described in the Bible is *Eros*. This is used to refer to romantic love. More explicitly, it refers to physical desire or longing. The second type of love is *Philos*. Philos is the sort of love that you have between a brother or sister or friends. It can be felt between those who share similar experiences or platonic affection for one another. The last is the type of love is the kind of love that Jesus demonstrated. It is called *Agape*. Agape love can be characterized as an all-encompassing way to love others. It refers to a general affection toward people, charitability, and benevolence. Benevolence is a word mostly used in church circles as charitable giving. However, a synonym for benevolence is compassion. Compassion is about action. When we witness suffering, we could respond with pity, which is really only that we acknowledge they are suffering. Or, we could go a step further, which gives way to sympathy or feeling bad about the fact that a person is suffering. Still, another step on the continuum might be that we empathize with those who suffer. Empathy is something that helps us connect with and share the feelings of others. However, what Jesus is asking us to do and modeled for us is compassion. Compassion is what compels us to act in order to remove someone's suffering.

In Matthew 22:37-40, Jesus responds to a Pharisee who asked what the greatest commandment was. Jesus replied to love God and love people. However, in John 15:12, Jesus again, raises the stakes and tells his disciples, "My command is this: Love each other as I have loved you." Now that we know how love is defined, the next question we must ask is, how did Jesus love? In the next verse (John 15:13), Jesus explains, "Greater love has no one than this, that one lay down his life for his friends. You are my friends if you do what I command you." There are two parallels to this verse. The first, is a command to sacrifice one's selfish desires to serve Jesus, our friend, just as Jesus laid down His life for ours. This means we need to set aside our selfish ambitions and comforts to be all in for His mission: to make people disciples who live and act the way that He does. The second, is how we should serve one another. Jesus is pointing out that we honor Him by how we love others. When we love people in a way that is sacrificial by setting aside our needs in order to meet the needs of others, we love the way He did. To sacrifice something is to destroy it to fulfill a purpose. Jesus died for us so that we could be part of God's family. Because of this, we should leave each day manifesting His kingdom here on Earth by loving people the way He did. It is at the cross that He not only demonstrated His love for us, but also mercy and grace. He gave to us when we did not deserve these gifts. But, how often do we withhold helping others because of conscious or subconscious judgements related to whether a person deserves our love or not? If people see a homeless person, they may automatically assume that they are a drug addict or alcoholic and opt to not help them. Or, perhaps they are a charlatan who is there only to make a living. This way of thinking results in us refusing to investigate a need any further because we have predetermined their story and decided it isn't worth the investment. But Jesus did not withhold from us because the Gospel is an inclusive message where everyone is invited to participate no matter your history.

Jesus also stood for equality among people. He was radical and went against the culture when He released the oppression of race, gender, ethnicity, and socioeconomic status. During the time of the New Testament, religion was quite exclusive. It was only for the Jewish people and mostly centered around the male Jews. Women, for example, were to be at home and their primary role was to maintain the household. In fact, it was considered taboo for men to speak to women in public. One story, found in Luke 13:10-17, tells the story of Jesus healing a woman in the synagogue. She had been suffering for 18 years. Jesus saw her and called her to come forward to Him and healed her. When the Pharisees were upset that he had done this, Jesus went on to call her a "daughter of Abraham." This is significant because only the term "son of Abraham" had been used to refer to men who were under the covenant between God and the Jewish people. In making that statement, He was making it clear that women have an equal place in the family of God.

In the story of the Samaritan woman found in John 4:4-42, we see Jesus not only speak to a woman, but a Samaritan woman. Samaritans were considered unclean by the Jews; they would not have associated with them. In this story, Jesus not only speaks to her, but asks to use her dish to draw up water. To share a dish with a Samaritan would have been unheard of in the Jewish culture. Jesus went on to have a conversation with the woman and invited her to drink His "Living Water" and reveal to her that He is the Messiah. One could also say this is an example of Jesus crossing not only racial lines, but also socioeconomic lines. Given that this woman had been married five times, she likely was an outcast according to the culture at the time. However, Jesus chose her to reveal, for the first time, His identity as the Messiah. When the disciples arrived on the scene, they were shocked to see Him speaking to her. This encounter with Jesus changed her and she went on to tell her entire town about this experience and many of them became believers. This demonstrates Jesus's intentionality in including those who are marginalized.

Jesus also tells us to love those who don't love us. In Luke 6:32-36, Jesus says, "If you love those who love you, what credit is that to you? Even sinners love those who love them. And if you do good to those who are good to you, what credit is that to you? Even sinners do that. And if you lend to those from whom you expect repayment, what credit is that to you? Even sinners lend to sinners, expecting to be repaid in full. But love your enemies, do good to them, and lend to them without expecting to get anything back. Then your reward will be great, and you will be children of the Most High, because He is kind to the ungrateful and wicked. Be merciful, just as your Father is merciful." This is yet another example of how Jesus expects us to be radical in the way we love. He asks us to love those who don't deserve our love but yet, so often, we place expectations on our love. We allow our humanness and culture to teach us how to love others. Our culture tells us to look out for ourselves first. However, the Kingdom of God doesn't work that way. In Philippians 2:3-4, we read, "Do nothing out of selfish ambition or vain conceit. Rather, in humility value others above yourselves, not looking to your own interests but each of you to the interests of the others" (NIV). Paul is telling us to seek the interests of others to lay down our lives and our comfort for that of others. That even means giving up material possessions to those who may need it more. Therefore, we should not store up treasures here on earth but steward these treasures in the way that God asks us to without an expectation to receive anything back in return. There are many times that I work with people and their response is, "Thank you for helping me; I'll go to church next Sunday." This makes me sad that they feel as though they need to meet some external expectation or standard that if we help them they must come into the church. Church, we cannot hold love and ultimately salvation as ransom. We also must get past this idea of instant gratification. When we help someone, or love someone who isn't used to receiving love, they might not respond the way that we had hoped. If you get that twinge of disappointment, take time to reflect on how you felt about their response. And in that moment, be intentional about asking yourself the question, "Am I helping this person because I get something out of it, or because I am compelled to love them because Jesus does?" You have to remember the people you are helping may come from experiences and situations in which they weren't loved, or they have been hurt by the Church or society and there is an enormous amount of distrust. So, it's important to approach these situations from the perspective that you are simply planting seeds, and the secret to making those seeds grow and truly transforming people is love. Jesus said people will know that we are children of God by how we love one another. This again, hinges on the example of Jesus on the cross. Jesus paid our debt because we couldn't. He loved us even though we were sinners and lived in rebellion from God, and, in doing so, He was merciful. He chose to show compassion even though it was within His power and right to punish because He is holy.

The way that Jesus loves is difficult to wrap your brain around. It goes beyond our capacity to extend ourselves to the needs of others. Jesus knew that we couldn't do it within our own strength, so He sent the Holy Spirit. The Holy Spirit is the presence of God living in us. Galatians 5:22-23 says, "But the fruit of the Spirit [the result of His presence within us] is love [unselfish concern for others], joy, [inner] peace, patience [not the ability to wait, but how we act while waiting], kindness, goodness, faithfulness, gentleness, self-control. Against such things there is no law" (AMP). It is through the Holy Spirit that humans gain access to the one who is the very essence of love. It is God Himself. He lives among us and not only makes us holy through His indwelling in us but gives us access to the supernatural ability to care for others. The role of the Holy Spirit is to guide our thoughts so that they become like His thoughts.

Recently I was having dinner with my family and some friends and we were having a wonderful time eating, laughing, and sharing stories. When we left the restaurant, the energy was still high and we were looking at each other smiling, laughing, and enjoying one another's company. As I watched some of our group walking ahead of me to beat the rain, I noticed there were two men slumped over under an overhang in an attempt to not be rained on. As each person walked by these two men, it didn't appear that any of them had noticed the two men were there. In fact, it was almost intentional that they would divert their eyes so that they didn't have to acknowledge the brokenness that was before them. I felt at that moment the Holy Spirit stir inside of me to say, "See how they are overlooked?" That question struck my heart and made it ache for the thousands of people that are overlooked because we don't want to acknowledge their suffering. I don't think this is because we don't care about suffering, but I think it is either there is a judgement being made or a sense of fear or powerlessness to act. There is a story about Jesus when He was on His way to Jerusalem traveling with some of the people who had become followers as he preached. As Jesus approached the city, I imagine that the conversation was light, and people were excited to be with Him and about the newfound connection with God that brought meaning and purpose to their lives. But amidst all the celebration, Jesus noticed a funeral procession coming from the city. At that moment, His attention became locked on the mother who was crying out for the son she had just lost. He knew that her husband had also passed away previously and losing her son meant she had no family left. Despite what was going on around him, Jesus saw her. And, not only did He see her, He was moved to respond to her pain. His response was to simply tell this devastated mother, "Don't cry." Then, He went on to perform a miracle by raising her son from the dead. Just as Jesus was prompted to see this mother, it is the Holy Spirit that gently nudges us to go talk to someone or to call someone who needs our help. The Holy Spirit often highlights people in a crowd or leads us to be kind to someone. He provides guidance and wisdom in every situation on how we are to respond. We are not powerless to impact the problem of poverty, we just have to allow ourselves to be led by the Holy Spirit and obedient to what He tells us to do.

It is also by the Holy Spirit that we are emboldened to speak the truth and to spread the Gospel, to bring the Good News to the people who need restoration and love. When Jesus preached, He told the people to repent for the "Kingdom of Heaven is near."

There are two very important things to notice about that statement. The first is the word repentance, which means to change your mind. Jesus was telling people to change their behaviors and the way they thought about the world, themselves, and about God. He was again inviting them to participate in this family that God had designed and to become citizens of Heaven even while still here on Earth. The second thing to notice is that the "Kingdom of Heaven is near." As believers, we may read that statement and interpret it to mean that the Kingdom of Heaven is near: that it will soon come in time. Yet, I think what Jesus meant is that the Kingdom of Heaven was in close proximity to them through Him and the Holy Spirit. You see, our responsibility as the Body of Christ is to become ambassadors of Heaven (2 Cor. 5:20), so that those we come in contact with will also be able to experience Heaven here on Earth because ambassadors are appointed by the leader of the country they represent. This is a high-ranking role in which the person is living in a foreign land to serve as a diplomat and representative of the country they serve. Their role is to ensure the relationship between the country they represent, and their country of assignment remains intact. Also, while living in their assigned country, they usually are given a territory for which they control, such as an embassy. When someone enters into that territory, they can receive protection or immunity from the country that the ambassador represents because the ambassador not only represents their country but carries with them the power and authority of the one they represent. This is what Paul meant when he spoke about being an ambassador for Christ. We are to be that diplomat representing Him and His kingdom to the world. It is our responsibility to allow those who are being oppressed to come under our wing to be sheltered by the country we represent, Heaven. The Kingdom of Heaven is near because *we* are the Kingdom of Heaven when the Holy Spirit resides in us. We are to live under the reality that Jesus is the King of this world. Living in this manner vastly changes the way we behave and the way we think about everything.

Consider the Lord's Prayer in Matthew 6:9-13:

"Our Father, who is in heaven,
Hallowed be Your name.
Your Kingdom come, Your Will be done, On Earth as it is in Heaven.
Give us this day our daily bread.
And forgive us our debts, as we have forgiven our debtors
And do not lead us into temptation but deliver us from evil.
For Yours is the Kingdom and the power and the glory forever.
Amen."

As we say this prayer, we often look at it from the lens of, "Lord, let your Kingdom come in my life as it is in Heaven." However, that line is not a plea for Heaven to impact you, it is meant to bring Heaven to the world. Just as Jesus prayed, "On Earth as it is in Heaven," we are to be the vessels through which the Kingdom of Heaven comes to all the Earth. This should be the cry of our hearts because when we pray the Lord's prayer, we are saying, "Lord, you are holy above all else and we want to walk in your good and perfect will for us and those we serve. We trust you to provide all that we need. Please forgive us and help us to forgive others. Teach us to live in a way that is pleasing to you so that your kingdom can be established here on Earth as it is in Heaven."

What Jesus did while here on earth was start a counter cultural movement to think about the needs of others. Jesus, our King, rules with self-sacrifice and love. Therefore, as a representative of His Kingdom, we should do the same. How can we claim we belong to Him, but misrepresent how He lived? James 2:16-17 says, "What good is it, my brothers and sisters, if someone claims to have faith but has no deeds? Can such faith save them? Suppose a brother or a sister is without clothes and daily food. If one of you says to them, 'Go in peace; keep warm and well fed,' but does nothing about their physical needs, what good is it? In the same way, faith by itself, if it is not accompanied by action, is dead" (NIV). So, you see it is imperative and integral to the message of love that we strive to meet the needs of people whether they are physical, emotional, or spiritual. By not addressing these things, we go against the example that Jesus demonstrated for us.

Early Christians sold all their possessions in order to serve the needs of those living in their community, as described in Acts 4:32-35, "All the believers were united in heart and mind. And they felt that what they owned was not their own, so they shared everything they had. The apostles testified powerfully to the resurrection of the Lord Jesus, and God's great blessing was upon them all. There were no needy people among them, because those who owned land or houses would sell them and bring the money to the apostles to give to those in need" (NLT). These early Christians realized that nothing they had come from themselves, and possessions and money were only tools used to further the business of the Father, which is to care for those in need.

During the Sermon on the Mount Jesus said, "You are the salt of the Earth; but if the salt has lost its taste (purpose), how can it be made salty? It is no longer good for anything, but to be thrown out and walked on by people [when the walkways are wet and slippery]. "You are the light of [Christ to] the world. A city set on a hill cannot be hidden; nor does anyone light a lamp and put it under a basket, but on a lampstand, and it gives light to all who are in the house. Let your light shine before men in such a way that they may see your good deeds and moral excellence, and [recognize and honor and] glorify your Father who is in Heaven. (Matthew 6:15-16, AMP). There is so much we could dive into related to this scripture. But, for the purposes of this chapter, there are a couple things to highlight. The first is that we are called to be the "salt of the Earth." But, what does that even mean? Salt has a few purposes; the first is to flavor food. I think we can all agree that salt makes most things taste better. So, by being salt, Jesus is telling us to make the world better by sticking to His purpose, which Jesus explains in Luke 6:18-19, "The Lord's Spirit has come to me, because he has chosen me to tell the good news to the poor. The Lord has sent me to announce freedom for prisoners, to give sight to the blind, to free everyone who suffers, and to say, 'This is the year the Lord has chosen" (CEV). The second use for salt is to purify. To prepare kosher foods as most Jews still do today, you put the item in salt and water and the salt draws the impurities out. It isn't abrasive and doesn't cause deterioration; it simply uses its nature to attract and soak up the impurities such as toxins and blood in meat. Isn't that exactly what the work of the cross and the Holy Spirit is about? To draw out those things that are not good in us? But, He does this in a way that is gentle and changes us from the inside out. Lastly, salt is used to preserve. The word *preserve* means to maintain a purpose in spite of difficulty, obstacles, or discouragement, and to continue steadfastly. Jesus certainly does this for us. He holds us up when we need comforting and strength. He gives us wisdom in every circumstance. This is also what we need to be doing for those we serve. If we stop doing this or being the "salt of the Earth," we are no longer useful for our primary purpose and must instead be used for secondary purposes, which are lesser in the Kingdom of Heaven. Because as He goes on to say, it is our good deeds that bring glory to the Father. It is our deeds that shine before all men, and it is in these good deeds that they come to recognize His Kingship. How we live our lives has a direct impact on people finding purpose, righteousness, faith, and salvation.

Reflection

Read 1 John 4:10-12, 19-21

Take some time to journal about the ways that God has shown His love for you. Then, ask God to reveal to you how He wants you to express that love to others.

Prayer

Father, you have been so generous to me. You love is never ending and never failing. Thank you for loving me. Help me to express this love to others that I encounter. Speak to me about how I can love others more as I go about my day. In Jesus Name, Amen.

Chapter 5

*"It is a tragedy when the church saves money instead of saving souls.
We must spend to save."*

— Reinhard Bonnke

In the Western Church, there is a great misunderstanding and misalignment of resources because we believe that what we earn belongs to us and it is up to us to decide how it is used. There is also a misunderstanding that responsible stewardship of money means the same thing as diligently saving it. In actuality, everything we have either as individuals or as a church organization is from God and belongs to God. Stewardship, according to the Holman Bible Dictionary, is "utilizing and managing all resources God provides for the glory of God and the betterment of His creation." So, if resources are meant to glorify God and the betterment of His creation, there are two questions we should ask: Who decides how those resources should be used? And, what are the missed opportunities to use those resources to better creation (i.e. our communities)? At the heart of these questions lies the plague that has run rampant in our churches for decades: a lack of trust in God. Even though the Bible clearly states in Proverbs 3:5, "With all your heart you must trust the Lord and not your own judgment" (CEV). Scripture also tells us God is trustworthy in Psalm 9:10, "Those who know your name trust you because you have not abandoned any who seek you, Lord" (CEB). You see, what I think is at the core of the church organization's way of managing money is that we are afraid when we need money we won't have enough. This mentality prevents us from making heavenly investments such as supporting those living in poverty. Because some church organizations do not have an understanding of whose resources they are stewarding and are not asking God how to use those resources, there is a misalignment between how we use them and God's vision and strategy for their use. We don't know how He wants us to use them because we simply don't ask Him. Instead, we do things like construct buildings that accrue debt and then ask God to bring provision for the debt even though we are clearly told to be lenders and not borrowers (Proverbs 22:7). What we should be doing is asking God, "What do you want us to do?" and then await His instructions for the strategy, when to move forward, and the resources to make it happen.

If you were to observe the financial practices of the church organization today, you may find most churches have a few things in common. The first is a push for congregants to tithe regularly. Those tithes are then distributed across operations, equipment, salaries, and practical needs to run ministries. Some churches may have charitable giving such as food pantries or clothes closets, but support for those outward-facing ministries is most often paid for by offerings, which are monies, fundraisers, or donations collected either outside of the tithing process or as a special needs request posed to the congregation. However, I would like you to consider shifting your perspective from doing the business of the church to tuning into what God wants us to do with our resources. There is nothing wrong with using funds from tithes to cover operational expenditures, but we should ask the Lord how He wants to distribute financial resources and be cautious to not divert them all to these fixed expenditures so we do not neglect caring for our people and communities.

Before ministries can be put in place to care for the poor, we have to realign our thoughts with God's thoughts, specifically as they relate to money. It is true money is needed to accomplish almost everything in the world we live in. So much so, I would venture to say this is an idol even in the church organization. We put our security in the amount of tithes collected and the bottom line of our bank account. But, Jesus told us to not store up treasures in Heaven, but to instead put our faith in our Father. He even warns us we cannot serve both God and money (Matthew 6:24-34). How can we be bold and radical like Jesus when our mindset about money is tarnished by the status quo?

The History of the Tithe

The first mention of a tithe was when Abraham gave the priest Melchizedek a tenth of the spoils (Gen. 14:20). But, we do not actually see the word tithe used until Leviticus 27, or approximately 600 years later. The first tabernacle, or what I would call the first "church" structure, was built by Moses during the Exodus. In Exodus 25, we read that God told Moses to collect an offering to go towards building the sanctuary. "Then the Lord spoke to Moses, saying, 'Tell the children of Israel to take an offering for me. From every man whose heart moves him [to give willingly] you shall take my offering. This is the offering you are to receive from them: gold, silver, and bronze, blue, purple, and scarlet fabric, fine twisted linen, goats' hair, rams' skins dyed red, porpoise skins, acacia wood, [olive] oil for lighting, balsam for the anointing oil and for the fragrant incense, onyx stones and setting stones for the [priest's] ephod and for the breast piece. Have them build a sanctuary for me, so that I may dwell among them. You shall construct it in accordance with everything that I am going to show you, as the pattern of the tabernacle and the pattern of all its furniture'" (Ex. 25:1-9, AMP). The sanctuary God asked Moses to build was to be His house so He could come and dwell among His people and provided a place for people to come and worship. It is important to note that Moses did not come up with the plan for what he thought the sanctuary should look like and then ask God for all the materials and skilled workers he needed to accomplish it. The vision for the sanctuary came after Moses had communion with God, during which he waited and listened to what God wanted to tell him. God simply told Moses to take up an offering. He wanted only those gifts from those who were moved in their hearts to give because those were pure offerings. He told Moses what items he should accept as offerings. Then, God told him what He wanted Moses and the Israelites to do with the offerings. God did not ask Moses to command each person to give a percentage of what was needed because He cares more about the condition of the heart than the actual gift; this is why He only wanted gifts, or offerings, from those who give cheerfully out of devotion to Him. However, when Moses came down from the mountain after meeting with God, he found the Israelites entrenched in sin and worshipping the golden calf (Ex. 32). It isn't until Exodus 35 that we see the construction on the sanctuary actually began. The Israelites had grown impatient waiting on God and decided to take matters in their own hands by worshipping Baal. Just like the Israelites experienced, taking things into our own hands can create unneeded delay, debt, difficulties, and strife. But, once the work the Lord commanded for the tabernacle began, they found that not only did they have enough offerings and skilled workers to build the Lord's sanctuary, there was an abundance. The skilled workers had to ask the Israelites to stop bringing their offerings because "the material they had was sufficient to do all the work, and more" (Ex. 36:5-7, ESV).

However, as we make our way through Scripture into Numbers and Deuteronomy and eventually Nehemiah, we find God changed the purpose or use of the tithe. In Numbers, God instructed the Israelites to give all of their tithes to the Levites to compensate them for all the work they had done to maintain the tabernacle. And, the Levites were to take a tenth of a tenth of the tithe given to them to provide for the priests. In Deuteronomy, the Lord told the Israelites to take all of their tithes, which in their time would most likely be crops, grain, and livestock, to the place God would show them. Then, God told them to eat the tithe in His presence so they could celebrate and rejoice for the blessings in the provisions God had given them. He asked them to do this so they would learn reverence and to worship God, who had provided for them. This is such a beautiful example of God's character and generosity. He asked them to set aside a time so they could come and be in His presence because He wanted to spend time with them. And, as a loving Father, He showed them He is their provider, He is holy, and He is worthy of their reverence and worship.

God also instructed the Israelites to take the tithe every third year and provide for the Levites, strangers, and the widows and orphans so they could eat and be satisfied. We then see in 2 Chronicles 31 that God instructed the Israelites to bring the tithes to the Levites, but there was such an abundance of the tithe had accumulated into piles and heaps. The Levites had too much and this is where we see the beginnings of the building of the storehouses. I think it's important to pause here for a moment and recognize a couple things. While the tithe is mandated, it is mandated in such a way that it provides for God's people and those who are serving Him through ministry, either as a Levite caring for the tabernacle or the priests who performed the rituals. Again, we see even though the Israelites were asked to provide only a tenth of their grain and produce, their tithes grew to such an amount there was more than what was needed to provide for the Levites and priests.

You can see how God was teaching the Israelites very important lessons along the way as it relates to the tithe. First, giving is meant to be cheerful and out of devotion to Him. Then He taught them to care for each other. Next, He instructed them to use the tithe to teach them about caring for those who took care of His house and performed the priestly duties. Lastly, he taught them to use the tithe to care for those who could not care for themselves such as orphans and widows. But, He didn't ask them to do this by stretching this finite amount of 10%; He blessed them beyond measure so that as He blessed them so would the tithe be increased. How often do we lack the faith that God will provide in such a way? In our own limited wisdom and understanding, we see a dollar amount and then we restrict what we do based on the dollars available. We have a tendency to only imagine what we think is possible. But, Jesus said, "With God all things are possible" (Matt. 19:26, NIV).

We also prioritize the needs of the church organization and don't seek to expand how we use our resources to care for the needs of people or worse, remembering and celebrating with Him for how He has provided. Therefore, our practice as church organizations should be to first ask the Lord what He wants to accomplish and be obedient in trusting His plan by doing what He asks of us and our churches.

We now find ourselves in the well-known passage regarding tithes found in Malachi 3. Oftentimes, I hear church leaders and pastors refer to the church as a storehouse. Every Sunday before introducing the time to take up tithes and offerings, this passage is often referenced: "'Bring the whole tithe into the storehouse, that there may be food in my house. Test me in this,' says the Lord Almighty, 'and see if I will not throw open the floodgates of Heaven and pour out so much blessing that there will not be room enough to store it'" (Mal. 3:10, NIV). We love to quote this verse to remind people that God commands that we bring our 10% to the church. Then, we tell people if they bring their tithe, they will be blessed according to how much they give. However, if we look at this verse in the context of the entire book of Malachai, we see God is actually not upset they aren't bringing a tithe, but is upset they are not giving with the right heart and not of their first fruits. Further, he admonishes the priests for allowing their behavior to continue and not holding the people accountable. In verse 5, He says, "'At that time I will put you on trial. I am eager to witness against all sorcerers and adulterers and liars. I will speak against those who cheat employees of their wages, who oppress the widows and orphans, or who deprive the foreigners living among you of justice, for these people do not fear me,' says the Lord of Heaven's Armies'" (NLT). God was also angry they were not caring for those who could not care for themselves. This included both those people who would see suffering and not act as well as those people who caused suffering for others. When I read this and think about most Western churches, it is hard for me to see the difference between us and the Israelites. We are still collecting tithes, but we do not have a culture built around the tithe being worship, and neglect what is important to God— taking care of people.

In Chapter 3 of Malachai, God goes on to chastise the Israelites for robbing Him of the tithe and He tells the priests to have the people bring the tithe to the storehouse. In the Malachai passages, God addresses the Israelites, His chosen people, to reprimand them for not giving their best to Him. The Israelites tried to deceive Him and disgrace Him by offering less than desirable sacrifices because their hearts were not in it. The issue wasn't that God wasn't getting the sacrifices, it was the half-hearted approach to the tithe that upset Him. Giving because you have to give isn't the heart posture God desires. He wants us to give in such a way that shows our reverence, devotion, and love for Him. The word robbed (or in some translations cheated) referenced in Malachi 3:8 is qaba in Hebrew (Strongs H6905). The literal translation of this word is "to cover." It is used to describe someone having a cup but covering the top with a hand so the wine pourer can't fill the cup. The application to this situation is that God is saying the act of not giving their best is covering the cup He wants to fill: the storehouse, or, in our case, the church organization. When we stop covering the cup by being generous, cheerful givers, God will fill our cup by pouring out so much blessing we can't contain it; the blessings will overflow. Conversely, if we continue to be ungenerous to those in need, or cover the cup, we block the blessings God has for us. You may think these passages speak to the individual Israelites. However, the message Malachai received from the Lord isn't directed only towards individuals. But, God also chastised the priests who were responsible for using the tithes brought forth. It is important for church leaders to understand that tithes and offerings should be used in a way that is pleasing to God and for the things God prioritizes. By not being radically generous with the resources entrusted to us or asking God how to use the resources He has given, we are covering the cup of blessing God has for our churches. It is also the responsibility of the leaders of the church organization to demonstrate and teach the heart of God to people.

In Matthew 23:23, we read about Jesus rebuking the Pharisees. He scolded them for paying their tithe but neglecting justice and mercy. Throughout all of Chapter 23, Jesus gives examples in which the Pharisees were doing the required rituals, but neglecting the things of the heart. Jesus was calling them out for the hypocrisy of keeping up outward appearances, but not understanding the heart of God. In many ways, the church organization today has fallen into the same mentality as the Pharisees. We encourage our congregants to pay the tithe and offerings, yet we're not stewarding those things to do to what God deems important such as justice and mercy. I find the current way of approaching finance in the church organization is flipped from that of Scripture. It is not uncommon to see the standard of practice amongst churches is to prioritize expenses such as securing a building for which they're in debt, rather than allowing the Lord to provide resources and wait on Him to give instructions for how they should be used. Just as the aforementioned Pharisees, we are putting our efforts into outward appearances like equipment and events, instead of prioritizing things that matter such as missional activities that help people, specifically those in our own communities. As we continue to look through the New Testament in Galatians and Romans, we see some early Christians sold everything they had and gave it to the church. We should be ready and willing to be "all in" no matter what "all in" looks like. Whatever God asks of us, whether it be our time, talent, or possessions (money, houses, cars, etc.), we should make available for His work.

We Live in a Kingdom

We must shift our perspective from identifying ourselves as citizens of the Earth to citizens of the Kingdom of Heaven in order to be "all in" for what God may ask us to do. The reality of living in a kingdom requires a radical change in the way we think because we are used to living in a democracy. Therefore, we cannot talk about the Kingdom without discussing government. When you live in a kingdom, life is much different than what we are used to. For example, there is a sovereign or a supreme ruler. This person dictates everything that happens within the kingdom. There is an agreement between the sovereign and the people residing within the kingdom. If they are a good sovereign, they make sure the people within the kingdom are protected and that the infrastructure is in place to distribute resources to those in need. In return, the subjects pledged their loyalty to the sovereign and agreed to follow his decrees. As citizens of the kingdom, the people experience the benefits of the kingdom. As children of God and citizens of His Kingdom, He is our sovereign. And as such, we get to benefit from the blessings and promises made in Scripture such as salvation, grace, peace, joy, love, and even provision for our physical needs. In return, we make Jesus our Lord and walk in step with the Holy Spirit so we can follow Jesus' example.

Kingdoms are made up of principalities, or states that fall within the kingdom, but are ruled by those given authority over a specific region. It is the responsibility of those put in charge of these principalities to represent the king. The church organizations are the vice regents of these principalities (we will talk about territory later). The role of a vice regent is to represent the king in their designated territory, which means they are the executor of the king's will in their principality. This practically looks like promoting the culture of the kingdom, building infrastructure, and using the resources given by the king to fortify and expand the kingdom.

As a church organization, we must connect to our role as vice regents and become more disciplined about asking our King what his intentions are for our assigned territory so we can be led by Him to transform our cities one territory at a time. But, in order to do this, we have to be willing to let go of the control over the money in our coffers and trust our King to know what is best for us and those we have the privilege of serving. This may look like saving money to expand your church building or it may look like using those savings to invest in the community. The point is that we need to shift from deciding for ourselves to asking the King what He wants done with the resources we have.

I think one way we can connect to the heart of Jesus is to be generous with the blessings He has given us in order to care for those He has entrusted to us: the pastor or staff He appointed to care for our churches, those within our church who need financial assistance, and the poor outside of our church so we can build the Kingdom in our communities. Just as in the nation of Israel during the times of Malachi, we too need a change of heart, to shift from being focused on checking the boxes of the Law (half-heartedly doing what is expected of us) in order to earn God's approval to having a heart for things God loves. We must get away from the mindset as individuals and as a church organization that any money or material things we have are ours in the first place. In James 1:17-18, James writes, "Whatever is good and perfect is a gift coming down to us from God our Father, who created all the lights in the heavens. He never changes or casts a shifting shadow. He chose to give birth to us by giving us His true Word. And we, out of all creation, became His prized possession" (NLT). Therefore, to become bold, generous, and even courageous in giving to others, we must accept nothing belongs to us because everything we have belongs to God and we are simply privileged to hold His resources until He tells us they are needed somewhere else.

The Limitless Supply of the Kingdom

We saw in the building of the first tabernacle God set forth a vision for the people so He could come and live among them. Then God said only use the offerings from the people who are moved in their hearts to give, which resulted in them receiving more than what was needed. Moses didn't say to God, "I bought this tabernacle, so God you need to provide the finances to pay off this loan." Proverbs 22:7 says, "The poor are ruled by the rich, and those who borrow are slaves of moneylenders" (CEV). Many church organizations have become slaves to their buildings. They are expensive to purchase and leave the church organization in debt for many years, which diverts finances away from investing in the work of ministry. The consequence is that trade-offs are made for spending; for example, we pay the mortgage instead of funding ministries. We have been programmed by our worldly culture to think "this is the way it is done" so we don't question how this aligns with the Word of God. Instead, imagine all churches are debt free and all money could be used for building the Kingdom. Scripture says, "No one can serve two masters. For you will hate one and love the other; you will be devoted to one and despise the other. You cannot serve God and be enslaved to money" (Matt. 6:24, NLT). When we borrow money from lenders, we are putting our trust in the lender to be our provider instead of the Lord. In doing this, have we slipped, even unknowingly into making money our God?

How we think impacts our behavior. If we have an unhealthy and non-Kingdom perspective about things like money and resources, then our behavior will reflect that perspective. How we think is largely shaped by our upbringing, experiences, and core beliefs. This is true even of how we think about money and the future and how we relate to others and think about ourselves. There are three categories of mindsets that help shape the way we view the world and they are based on socioeconomic status: poverty, middle-class, and wealthy.

Many church organizations are living with the scarcity mindset of poverty despite the promise, "The Lord is my shepherd, I lack nothing" (Psalm 23:1, NIV). Can you imagine if the Church lived by this promise? There is nothing God will ask us to do that He won't provide for because His Kingdom and resources are limitless. If the church organization could adopt this mindset of limitless resources, they would no longer have to make decisions out of fear of not having enough money. This would help shift thinking from having to make things happen or find funds to support God's work to trusting in His vision and His ability to provide, which aligns us with what He asked of us in Matthew 6:33, "Seek the Kingdom of God above all else, and live righteously, and He will give you everything you need" (NLT). For those who have a poverty mindset, money is meant to be spent because their focus is on the present. Someone with a poverty mindset is thinking about what they need today and how they can get it. Practically, this looks like someone who gets their income tax check and spends it on clothes or a vacation versus paying off debt or saving it for the future. The person with a middle-class mindset, however, will take that money and save it because they value their ability to have a choice and to plan for the future. The wealthy person, on the other hand, recognizes money is a tool meant to invest to make more money while also saving for the future because their focus is on cultivating a legacy so their children are left with an inheritance.

We discussed in the second chapter the importance of hope not just skills to realize a better future. Those with a poverty mindset don't believe they have the power to change their circumstances. They believe they are a victim of the world around them and life is something to be endured. This looks like a church who perhaps has lost hope in strategizing for the future. They may have grown comfortable in their complacency or lack of growth. While those who identify with the middle-class mindset believe their grit makes them successful because it is based on their own ability to perform and achieve their desired future. As a church organization, this may look like a church who saves and saves every penny they receive because they are afraid they won't have enough when they need it. But, those with a wealthy mindset believe in noblesse oblige. Noblesse oblige is a French term that infers the responsibility of those who have wealth to be generous to those who are less privileged than they are. This explains why we see the wealthy starting charities and foundations. For the Church, noblesse oblige looks like churches who approach the management of their finances from a Kingdom perspective. They understand money is a tool that is meant to be invested because investment in people and communities has a huge return on investment from a Kingdom perspective. They also understand it is their responsibility to take ownership of the territory God has assigned to them.

Each of us has an internal motivation that propels us forward towards our goals for the future. If someone with a poverty mindset thinks money is to be spent and they are powerless to change their circumstances, it should not be a surprise the fear of not having what they will need is the driving force behind their decisions. They are driven to survive and because the pain of today can be tough to carry, they may look for ways to escape and cope. Whereas, someone with a middle-class mindset is driven by achievement and more specifically working hard to get there. This is where skill and hope are aligned. They are hopeful and have faith for the future, but believe the only way to get there is through their own works and conventional wisdom. While a person with a wealth mindset is driven by love—love for their family through legacy, love through connection to people, and love for their community through generosity.

Many churches fall into the poverty or middle-class mindset trap. If there is a poverty mindset for money in the church organization, it looks like money being spent without intention, but instead worrying about getting through the present moment or using the extra money this year to throw a party. If there is a middle-class mindset, then churches want to save all the extra money they have in case they need it for the future because there is only a finite amount of money available. However, with a wealthy mindset, all possibilities are endless because someone with a wealthy mindset doesn't worry about whether or not they will have access to money, which allows them to be more generous or practice noblesse oblige. They also recognize money is to be invested to create more wealth. The church should be practicing their inherent responsibility to be generous and understand that spending money on their community is a heavenly investment, not only in the community--but the eternity for those living in the community and ultimately the Kingdom of God. Understanding this concept is what leads to building a legacy of Kingdom expansion. Lastly, our internal motivation as believers and churches with a wealthy mindset is to gain and benefit from the financial, political (government of Heaven), and social connections we have to first the Father and secondly to each other as the Body of Christ. In order to make this shift from poverty or middle-class mindsets to a wealthy one, we must also know our identity. Just as we discussed in previous chapters, the root of poverty is a spiritual problem caused by a lack of knowledge of identity, and so it is with the Church and the church organizations.

From Orphans to Heirs

Earlier in this book I discussed poverty, at its root, as a spiritual problem caused by not knowing and living within our God-given identity. This same problem faced by those in poverty is also faced by the Church, which leads to why church organizations manage their finances the way they do. In the previous chapter, however, we discussed the difference between being an orphan and a son of God (sonship). However, another transition is still needed as it relates to identity and that is from sonship to heir. Tim Alley, a friend of mine who is the pastor of Baldwin Assembly of God in Baldwin, Michigan, describes the difference between these identities as this: "Orphans don't believe, sons do believe, heirs know God believes in them and has given them the Kingdom." Unless we understand this Kingdom is at our disposal to do the King's work, we will never become bold and radically generous. Pastor Tim further describes these identities in a way I think ties together the concepts focused on identity and mindsets in this table, which I have modified slightly to help visualize the connections between these concepts.

Identity	Orphan	Son	Heir
View of God	controlling	to be worshipped	one with Jesus
Mindset	slave or poverty mentality	Working class mentality	royal, wealthy mentality
Future	powerless, no control over their future	must earn and manage, prepare for the future	noblesse oblige
Internal motivation	Fear (lives in the flesh)	faith/hope	love
	Galatians 5:17	(crucified the flesh)	(living in the Spirit)
		Galatians 2:20, Hebrew 11:6	Romans 8:17, Matthew 6:33
How they think	defined by their past, doesn't pray; demands justice for themselves	defined by the Word; prays or needs; lives by grace	defined by the Spirit; prays to know God; lays life down for others
	(no justice comes or is ever enough)	(Received God's Justice, Salvation)	(Seeks justice for the lost)
Behaviors	Fear	Surrender	Fearless
	Worry	Cease Worrying	Content
	Anger	Peaceful	Peace Maker
	Complaining	Satisfied	Encourager
	Unforgiving	Forgiving	Takes no offense
	Hoarding, nothing is enough	Provided for (has enough)	Selfless, has more than enough
	Stealing	No Need	Generous
	Dishonesty	Speaks Truth	Prophesy
	Manipulation	Trusts	Obedience
	Issues with Authority	Submits to Authority	Ambassador for Authority
	Secrets/Hiding	Confesses Sin	Humble
	Insecure	Secure	Lives with abandon
	Alienated from God	Accepted	Lives in God's presence
View of themselves	Shame, guilt, hopelessness	shame & guilt free; great hope	carries God's glory; lives abundantly

What is depicted in this table is summed up in Romans 8:12-17, which reads, "Therefore, brothers and sisters, we have an obligation—but it is not to the flesh, to live according to it. For if you live according to the flesh, you will die; but if by the Spirit you put to death the misdeeds of the body, you will live. For those who are led by the Spirit of God are the children of God. The Spirit you received does not make you slaves, so that you live in fear again; rather, the Spirit you received brought about your adoption to sonship. And by Him we cry, 'Abba,

Father.' The Spirit himself testifies with our spirit that we are God's children. Now if we are children, then we are heirs—heirs of God and co-heirs with Christ, if indeed we share in His sufferings in order that we may also share in His glory" (NIV). This is the journey of the believer—to transition from being an orphan to becoming an heir. This is so that we not only understand who our Father is, but also to have a deep understanding of our position and resources. Those with an heir identity do not worry about whether or not they will have enough money or resources. In fact, scarcity isn't even a thought! People who are born into wealthy families understand what is at their disposal and their familial and social responsibilities. This is how not only the individuals within the Body of Christ must see themselves, but also the church organization. Church organizations have a responsibility to steward the resources given through tithes and offerings to utilize and manage these God-given resources for the glory of God and the betterment of His creation. It is also the responsibility of the church organization to demonstrate what it means to be an heir and vice regent of their territory so those within their house of worship may live in the same manner. God calls us to know our identity so we can live free in the Spirit. In doing so, we become radically generous, love unconditionally, live fearlessly, and are emboldened to carry the Kingdom to restore our cities.

Feed the hungry,
and help those in trouble.
Then your light will shine out from the darkness,
and the darkness around you will be as bright as noon.
The Lord will guide you continually,
giving you water when you are dry
and restoring your strength.
You will be like a well-watered garden,
like an ever-flowing spring.
Some of you will rebuild the deserted ruins of your cities.
Then you will be known as a rebuilder of walls
and a restorer of homes.
Isaiah 58:10-12

Reflection

Read Matthew 23

What point was Jesus making to the Pharisees? How do you think your church is the same or different?

Read Romans 8:12-17

Where do you think you are personally on your journey from orphan to heir? What about your church? In what ways do you think your church needs to make a change towards heir?

Prayer

Father, there is so much pain and suffering in our world, but I know you have brought me to this church and community for a reason. Show me how you would like to restore me, my church, and my community. Show me the brokenness in me and around me so that I may know every weakness that needs your strength. Elevate my thinking to that of the Kingdom and teach me what it means to be a co-heir with Christ. Show me how you want your Church to expand your Kingdom. Teach me to be fearless and bold in how we use the resources you have entrusted to us. In Jesus' name, Amen.

Chapter 6

"Faith begins with a backwards look at the cross, but lives with a forward look at the promises."
—John Piper

The idea of mobilizing the local church came to me during one of my quiet times with the Lord. I was asking Him about the purpose He has for my life. But, instead of just giving me an answer, the Holy Spirit asked me a series of questions:

Holy Spirit: How many churches do you think are in your community?

Me: I don't know. Maybe 200.

Holy Spirit: How many people do you think go to those churches?

Me: Maybe on average 100?

Holy Spirit: How many people is that total?

Me: 20,000

Holy Spirit: I wonder, how much an impact could be made for people who live there if everyone was intentional about helping people?

That conversation with the Holy Spirit was all it took. The lightbulb turned on in my brain (and my heart) and He downloaded a dream that I have been obsessed with ever since: mobilizing local churches to transform their cities. The ideas about how to do this just kept firing one by one in my mind. I could hardly write fast enough to capture all that He was showing me. Suddenly, I realized how all my work experience, schooling, and spiritual growth had brought me to this point. As a Christian, God had been showing me how to really love people and care for those who are unable to care for themselves. As a public health professional, I have gained knowledge about the social determinants of health, health disparities, and the complexities of poverty. And, as a quality improvement coach, I know how to systematically uncover root causes to problems, identify potential solutions, and measure for improvement post interventions. God had a plan for me to use all this knowledge and experience to support the Church in transforming our cities in measurable ways.

This book, so far, has focused on the many problems facing those living in poverty and the mindsets that exist within the Church that need to change in order to really make an impact in the cities we are supposed to be serving. However, in order to make a transformation, we need to define exactly what type of transformation we want to see occur. To do that, we need to get on the same page about what the Good News actually is. It seems so foundational, but there are many in the Church who think the Good News is just a "Get Out of Hell Free" card. But, the Gospel is so much more. When Jesus was crucified, He took on the weight of our sins so we can have open access to God. His resurrection became the invitation to become part of God's family. Accepting this invitation allows us to become part of the New Covenant in which we are forgiven for our sins and we receive the gift of grace despite our many transgressions. By saying "Yes" to Jesus' invitation, we are no longer living in rebellion from God, instead we are stepping into a union with Christ. This marks a moment that is pivotal for the believer because it is the catalyst of change from being who they were into being who Christ created them to be—a new creation. The concept of this new creation is described in Ephesians 4:22-24, "Regarding your previous way of life, you put off your old self [completely discard your former nature], which is being corrupted through deceitful desires, and be continually renewed in the spirit of your mind [having a fresh, untarnished mental and spiritual attitude], and put on the new self [the regenerated and renewed nature], created in God's image, [godlike] in righteousness and holiness of the truth [living in a way that expresses to God your gratitude for your salvation]" (AMP). Paul tells us in this passage that we have become a new person and the expression of that transformation is to live differently.

We should be overjoyed at this prospect. Praying the prayer of salvation isn't meant to be a "I'm going to Heaven " check box, but rather, it's a transformation of self. When I think of how great God's love for us is, I am overjoyed and overwhelmed by it. I can't comprehend it. I think about people in my life and how they have wronged or hurt me and how I have struggled to forgive them. But, Jesus forgave all that we have done, even before we asked or made amends, because His love transcends our transgressions. As I write, I struggle to find the words to describe the magnitude of that sacrifice. I find it difficult, at times, to accept that kind of love actually exists and that it is for me, and I don't think that is an experience unique to me. At the moment of salvation, we have an emotional response in which we feel the conviction of the Holy Spirit and realize we need Jesus to fill the empty void existing within us. That moment is wonderfully euphoric. In a split second, we release our sin and ask for forgiveness. It is replaced with a peace that we have never felt before because in that moment we experience pure freedom; freedom from the power of sin and even death. Unfortunately, many Christians' experience ends at this moment and their newfound freedom fades. I don't want to undermine the importance of salvation. It is the thing that draws us to Christ and repairs our relationship with God. However, just as grace is an unbelievable gift, so is abundance. God has more for us.

The Gospel is simple and yet very complex. If we do not fully understand the entire work of the cross, we can miss what Jesus actually died for. In John 12:47, Jesus says, "For I did not come to judge the world, but to save the world" (NIV). The word saved, used in this verse, in the Greek language is *sozo* (Strong's G4982). Typically, we translate that word to mean Jesus saves us from

Messianic judgement. However, there is more packed into that word. Sozo actually means to make well, heal, restore to health, or make whole. Jesus also said that He came to give life abundantly (John 10:10). This word abundance, *perissos* (Strongs G4053) in the Greek, means to exceed what is necessary or beyond measure. Lastly, Jesus is called the Prince of Peace (Isaiah 9:6). The word that is used in Scripture for peace in Hebrew is *shalowm* (Strongs H7965) and in the Greek is *eirēnē* (Strongs G1515). When we study the meaning behind these words, it brings richness to our understanding of why Jesus is the Prince of Peace. The words essentially mean to bring to completeness or restoration. A more literal translation might be "nothing missing, nothing broken." Jesus came so that He could bring shalowm and give us back what was lost or stolen after The Fall so our relationship with God could be made whole. But many of us might not fully understand the abundance we have received in Christ and, therefore, we don't access it because we don't understand or don't know how.

What does living a life of abundance look like? Is this something we can even comprehend? How does living an abundant life actually play out in real life? If we are going to help others live life abundantly, shouldn't we know what that looks like and live it ourselves? Schlyce Jiminez, founder of Emerge School for Transformation, defines this state of wholeness with what she calls the Seven Pillars of Wholeness:

The Spiritual Pillar - Refers to your spiritual health and wholeness, addressing things like your relationship with God and your identity in Christ.

The Mental Pillar - Refers to your intellectual and mental health, addressing things pertaining to your ways of thinking and need for mind renewal.

The Emotional Pillar - Refers to your emotional health, addressing things like your character and emotional maturity.

The Relational Pillar - Refers to the health of your relationships, addressing things like your ability to set boundaries, resolve conflicts, and develop and sustain healthy relationships.

The Financial Pillar - Refers to your financial IQ, addressing the ways that you think about money and how to best invest, save, give away, and spend your money.

The Physical Pillar - Refers to your physical health and wholeness, addressing things like divine healing and taking good care of your physical body.

The Vocational Pillar - Refers to your calling in life, addressing things like your career, your earning potential, your life purpose, and how you use your gifts to serve humanity.

Life in abundance means having wholeness in all the areas of your life and being aligned with God's promises for your life. It sounds much like the word shalowm doesn't it? This is why poverty is a spiritual issue. Poverty has to do with lack of wholeness. This is the reason we continue to put resource after resource into solving this problem. But, we are only applying a band aid to the symptoms of poverty if we don't address the root cause. Poverty, as I mentioned before, is not a lack of money: it is the lack of Jesus and, therefore, a lack of identity in Christ and the benefit of union with Him—wholeness. Further, unless there is a relational component to whatever support we provide to the underprivileged, we will continue spinning our wheels around solving the problem of poverty. Our goal should be nothing more than to help people rely on Jesus and not on individuals or systems. It is only through relying on Christ they experience wholeness. But, in order for us to help others experience wholeness, we ourselves need to understand what it is and demonstrate it.

The secular world, without knowing it, has developed a framework for identifying the areas that need to be in place for someone to be healthy, or what we in the Church would call living a life of abundance. In fact, the World Health Organization says "health is a state of complete physical, mental, and social well-being and not merely the absence of disease or infirmity." To understand why some people are healthier than others, researchers have developed a framework for what needs to be in place to live a healthy life. They call this framework the social determinants of health. They say that in order for someone to live a longer, healthier life, they need each of these things in place. When they are not in place, their health is impacted. There are six categories of determinants: economic stability, neighborhood and physical environment, education, food, community and social context, and healthcare system (see table).

Economic Stability	Neighborhood and Physical Environment	Education	Food	Community and Social Context	Health Care System
Employment	Housing	Literacy	Hunger	Social integration	Health coverage
Income	Transportation	Language	Access to healthy options	Support systems	Provider availability
Expenses	Safety	Early childhood education		Community engagement	Provider linguistic and cultural competency
Debt	Parks	Vocational training		Discrimination	
Medical bills	Playgrounds				
Support	Walkability	Higher education			Quality of care

Health Outcomes
Mortality, Morbidity, Life Expectancy, Health Care Expenditures, Health Status, Functional Limitations

Source: Kaiser Family Foundation

If these determinants are not in place, people live shorter lives, have more health problems, and experience functional limitations. In fact, the National Academy of Medicine states that 80% of health problems are caused from not having the social determinants in place. Looks a lot like the Seven Pillars of Wholeness doesn't it? Except it is missing the most important pillar that everything flows out of—Jesus. The world has tried and tried to address these things. We spend dollar after dollar on programs and research to tell us what we already know: Jesus is the answer to every single problem and it is through His Church that He fixes all problems. Poverty, or lack of wholeness, will never be solved if the Church is not intentional about addressing it.

The dream that God has shown me for the Church is that each and every believer would be moved by compassion, just as Jesus was and is, to help transform the lives of people. We transform cities by transforming people. I know that God is raising up leaders to look past the same old way of doing outreach based on events that are focused on fun and giveaways. Those things are not inherently bad, but it isn't enough. We should be investing in programs and resources that are more meaningful to communities. Things that could literally transform communities and build relationships with the people who live in them. When I look at this list of social determinants (which I will talk about in relation to addressing poverty in the communities because it is something that communities monitor and actually measure), I see things that could easily be addressed by the Church. After all, the Bible says that we should be all things to all people (1 Corinthians 9:22). To address economic stability, we could host job fairs and help people with creating resumes. For neighborhood and physical environment, we could do things to help fix rundown homes and run programs for kids to keep them in positive, safe, loving environments. We could impact education by offering tutoring and mentoring at-risk youths. Starting a food co-op and partnering with local food pantries could help increase access to food. To address community and social context, we should look for ways our churches can be focal points in our communities. And, for healthcare, we could host healthy cooking classes and partner with local health organizations to do dental exams or vaccination clinics.

This does lead me to another point which is that churches shouldn't put effort and resources into something because it sounds like a good idea. Take time to understand the needs of your community and the resources that are already available to meet those needs. More importantly, ask God to reveal to you the work that He wants you to do. It is great to have a food closet, but if there are 25 other food closets in your community it may be best to focus on providing for the community in another way. One way you can better understand the needs of those you serve, is to look up your local health report through your community health department or local hospital. They are required to do one every three years and it is available for the public to access. If we, the Church, can start looking at the social determinants in our community and being intentional about addressing them, we will really start to see things change.

However, what makes us different from every other organization is we will also be sharing the Gospel with people who need to know they are deeply loved by a caring and good Father. Don't forget you are an ambassador of Christ. You carry the peace and abundance you have access to because of who you are in Christ.

If you are an individual reading this book and aren't currently responsible for developing outreach programs, pray for God to use you to be a blessing to others. Don't just meet an immediate need for an individual and move on, but know you helping that person is a divine appointment and the opportunity to build a relationship with someone because after all, God is all about relationship. Most often, it is not just one need that someone has. And I would venture to say it most often is not just a physical need, but a spiritual, emotional, or relational need that is more critical. Additionally, be a voice for those who are oppressed. Social determinants are also impacted by structural factors like policies put in place by the government. Proverbs 31:8-9 says, "Speak up for those who cannot speak for themselves, for the rights of all who are destitute. Speak up and judge fairly; defend the rights of the poor and needy" (NIV). As an individual, stay informed and write your officials to lobby for change that supports those who cannot support themselves. Additionally, ask the Lord to help you better care for those who are ostracized such as for those who experience inequalities because of race, sexual orientation, gender, or socioeconomic status. The Gospel and the promises that come with it are for everyone. As a Church, some of us have not done a good job of loving those from these groups of people.

For all of us, the most effective thing we can do is to begin praying for our communities. Our prayers are powerful and they can change what is happening in the physical realm. If you are going to start anywhere, start here. There are many things to pray for like: strong families, new companies to come into your area that bring new jobs, eradication of addiction and crime, and teachers and school administrators to have divine favor when applying for grants to provide more programs to the kids they teach, to name a few. Together, as the Body of Christ, we can transform our cities. We can be an army fueled by love that rises up to crush the schemes of Satan that cause oppression and poverty in our communities.

Reflection

Read through the pillars of wholeness. How has wholeness (or lack of wholeness) been demonstrated in your life?

Ask the Lord about what areas He wants to heal in your life and write them in your journal. Write a declaration of healing for yourself for those areas. Display that declaration somewhere you will see it daily and read it aloud each day.

Next, journal about how you can help others in their journey towards wholeness. How could you or your church help those in need in your community?

Prayer

God, you are my healer. Holy Spirit, show me the areas in my life that aren't aligned with your promises for me. Reveal to me your truth and the lies I have been believing in those areas of my life. Show me ways that I can extend your peace, the kind that brings wholeness, to others. In Jesus Name, Amen.

Chapter 7

"With man this is impossible, but with God all things are possible."
— *Matthew 19:26*

When I was in college, my professor asked me to do an assignment. The assignment was to review the various social determinants of health and reflect on what role they had in my life. This assignment was difficult emotionally. He asked me to remember and think about situations that, honestly, I had suppressed for a long time. I hadn't realized what a profound impact these things had on my life. Using my own life experiences, I want to provide a case study to demonstrate how all the things we have been discussing in this book connect together. I would like to share my story so that we can begin to connect the dots between social determinants and being moved by compassion to care for others.

For much of our childhood, my three siblings and I grew up with both parents. I was the oldest. I had what to me felt like a normal childhood. My parents both worked, but weren't able to make ends meet. As a result, that often meant we moved around a lot. Our first place was in a Section 8 apartment complex. Section 8 housing is for individuals and families who live below the poverty line. As a kid, living in this apartment complex was great because the apartment buildings surrounded a large field where all the kids from the neighboring apartments could play. I lived there before I was in kindergarten and I remember being able to play and roam around by myself with my siblings and a cousin who lived in an apartment adjacent to us. There were times when we would have to really stretch our food to make it. My mom and aunts had been in foster care, so once my mom was of age she took in her youngest sister so that she could live with us. I loved having my aunt live with us. She was around 17 years old at this time and always played with me and read to me. While we lived in Section 8 housing, my dad got a job working in a factory. This meant that we made too much money to continue living in low-income housing. When I was old enough to attend kindergarten, my parents decided we would move in with my grandparents. It was important to them that we attended the same school they had attended, and they needed my grandparents to help take care of us while they worked. My grandparents had a family room on their second floor so my parents, siblings, and I lived in that room. Most days my siblings and I spent our time with our friends riding bicycles, building forts, and walking trails in the woods or cornfields near where we lived. It was during this time that a new family, the Carters, moved into the neighborhood. They quickly became our friends, especially my mom and Mrs. Carter. It wasn't long after meeting the Carters that they invited us to attend church with them. While my mom and dad had attended church growing up, this was the first time we had attended church as a family. My mom didn't always attend regularly for a lot of reasons. She often worked in the evenings and was going to college at this point. I think this is important to point out as you begin to work with families. Even though people might have the desire or best intentions to attend services and get involved, they may just not be at a point in their life that they are able to. We were lucky that we had my grandparents and the Carters to take us.

Between kindergarten and fifth grade, we moved three more times. There were many reasons for that. One of the homes was rent to buy, but when the owner wanted to sell my parents did not have the means or the credit to get a loan for a mortgage. The only home we could afford to move to, while in the same school district, was away from my grandparents and the Carters which felt isolating. Also, because of geography, we weren't able to get to church as often. But, due to the rent being raised, we were forced to move again. This time, we were able to move back into the neighborhood with the Carters and my grandparents. We were in this new home for a short time before there was a major shift in our family unit. When I think about my childhood, I remember fondly the time I spent with my siblings. I have many happy memories that we made together. However, there was a lot of conflict happening between my parents.

When I was in fifth grade, my parents told us that they were getting a divorce. I think of this sort of like the dark ages for my childhood. Suddenly, that security was ripped from us in this single decision. After they told us they were getting divorced, things moved quickly. There was a lot more arguing in my home. My parents were furious with each other and there was a lot of arguing about who would get us and how often we would see the other one. I remember feeling scared. Because my dad was moving out, my mom could no longer afford the house we were living in so we moved again. It was only down the street but it was across a major highway which doesn't seem like we were moving very far away, but it did create a barrier for us to connect with our neighborhood friends and grandparents. We again were feeling isolated. I was entering middle school by this time and as you can imagine for most tween-age girls this added its own stressors and challenges. Now, I was beginning to feel the division and the isolation of being in middle school. Suddenly, the girls who I had been friends with in elementary school began to form cliques. Unfortunately, while I had some friends, from the perspective of the popular girls, I didn't have the *right* kind of friends. I wasn't a nerd by any means, but I also wasn't in the cool crowd. That opened me up to being bullied. But, I was lucky because I was still making it to church, which meant that even if my school hours weren't comforting I knew I had friends there who I could count on.

My mom was working three jobs at this time, so she was gone during the day at her normal job and then nights and weekends for her other two jobs. Even with how hard she worked, it was never enough to make ends meet. The car would inevitably break down or we would fall behind in the utility bills because she hadn't made enough money to pay the rent. There was always this game of shuffling around resources, "borrowing from Peter to pay Paul" so to speak. It was often that I would come home from school and there would be nothing in our refrigerator or our cupboards. Bread and butter were typically my meal of choice. I am glad that I was able to get free lunch at school so I did have some food to eat, but it was always embarrassing to me to have to stand in that line: the poor kids line. I was thankful that my grandmother and my aunt worked at that school. They were so kind to pay for me to have the premium lunch. They didn't know how I felt about having to stand in that line. I was especially thankful that they were there when my mom took on her third job and we made too much money to get free lunch. Because for me, that meant that I would go without breakfast and lunch. Some nights we went to my grandparents' house and so we were able to get food there. However, there were days that I wasn't able to get any meals for one reason or another. This was because of how either my grandparents or aunt's schedule worked out or we weren't going to my grandparents that evening, which would mean I would have to eat the food my friends didn't finish sometimes. Even as I write this, tears well up because of the shame and isolation I felt because I did not fit in with the other kids. We were fortunate that from time to time people who attended churches that had food closets would randomly drop food off to us when things got really bad. I remember during holidays we would receive free food and delivery of Christmas gifts. I didn't have the things that other kids had. Clothes we're also a big deal at that age. I didn't always have cool clothes and had to rely on my friends to let me borrow what they had. I was fortunate because cleanliness was very important in my family. My mom always made sure that we had clean clothes to wear. Once, these things had been not as noticeable to me because of my age but they magnified when my parents got divorced.

It was at this point in my life I started to make different choices in my friends. I wanted to hang out with the cool kids and go to their parties. I wanted to feel accepted by them. I was bullied because I was "too" good, so I wanted to stop being good. So, I started sneaking out of the house, smoking, and going to parties. But, there was a limit to how far my conscience would let me go. I now know that it was the voice of the Holy Spirit that stopped me from making bigger mistakes, but it felt like my whole life was in shambles. My mom and I fought all the time. I was angry and sad and scared about our life circumstances, but at that time, I didn't know how to communicate that to anyone so it played out in my actions and attitude.

While this isn't my entire story, it is enough to paint a picture and there were other issues within my home. Not only did we have to cope with what it was like to be in poverty, there were also issues within our home related to substance abuse, mental illness, and physical and emotional abuse. Both my parents had issues that they were dealing with from their childhood that played out in how they treated each other and us kids. I know now that they were doing the best they could with what they had, but throughout my life, those things had a lasting effect on me. How could they possibly be able to manage and cope with all the things that had been stacked up against them? Given my family history, it would have been very easy for my family to become a statistic like so many who are living in poverty. Below is a table of social determinants and my experiences:

Social Determinant	My Experiences
Economic Stability *Poverty* *Employment* *Food Insecurity* *Housing Instability*	Grew up in a single-parent home Socioeconomic status was between working poor to the poverty level Food insecurity We were forced to move every 1-2 years for various reasons My mom was gone a lot because she worked several jobs and went to school
Education *High School Graduation* *Enrollment in Higher Education* *Language and Literacy* *Early Childhood Education and* *Development*	I have a large family and only four of us are college-educated (mom and dad's side combined) I was enrolled in free, government-supported preschool program (Head Start); I remember people coming to the house to do home visits I did well in high school Obtaining a college education was arduous because of financial constraints
Social Community Context *Social Cohesion* *Civic Participation* *Perceptions of Discrimination and* *Equity* *Incarceration*	I grew up in a single-parent home and my dad was not involved Involved in my church community I experienced embarrassment because I couldn't do and have the things that others did so it instilled a belief that I was inferior to others, especially those who had money
Health and Healthcare *Access to Health Care* *Access to Primary Care* *Health Literacy*	I remember having access to healthcare, but dental care was hit or miss; cleanings were covered, but any dental work was not I have a high level of health literacy
Neighborhood and Built *Environment* *Access to Healthy Foods* *Quality of Housing* *Crime and Violence* *Environmental Conditions*	I lived in a rural area, which limited my ability to participate in extracurricular activities in my community I only had access to the food that my grandparents prepared or people gave us, which was not always healthy I always had a safe, clean home I did not live in a violent area Many of my peers drank at an early age and used substances

My Adverse Childhood Events score would be an 8 out of 10. This means that I had a much higher risk than the general population for chronic disease, difficulty holding a job, and mental illness. As I moved into adulthood, I did have some of these things play out in my life. During my teen years, I had gone between anorexia and bulimia. I had attempted suicide by taking a bottle of pills. I struggled with chronic depression and anxiety for most of my life. I had difficulty in relationships because I didn't know how to process emotions and resolve conflict, as I had never learned how to do so. As I moved into adulthood, I went through hills and valleys of working at being healthy and returning to negative habits. I began to cling to the things that I could control since my life up until that point had been chaotic and out of my control. This translated to obsessively worrying about my health by rigidly tracking calories and excessively exercising. Then, to counteract this desire to be in control, I turned to addictive habits like smoking and abusing alcohol to feel relaxed and to decompress. In some ways, the effects of living in poverty still exist in my life. However, God is faithful. He has brought me this far and so I know He will continue to do good work in me.

As I went through the list of social determinants for my assignment and listing my experiences, I began to notice something very profound. While we did receive assistance from the government by way of welfare, Head Start and Section 8 housing and my mom received a Pell Grant to be able to go to college, it wasn't just the programs we qualified for that changed our lives: it was the people. My mom worked a lot to keep our heads above water. We were fortunate to have my grandparents and aunts to provide childcare so my mom could finish her college education. My mom had friends who would hire her to do housework or party planning for them so that she didn't have to feel like she was getting a handout. If our car would break down, my grandparents would find a way to get it fixed. We also had friends who would get food donations or gifts at Christmas from their churches and deliver them to us. One of our neighbors sent my mom $25 every week. Another family from our church owned a ranch and meat packaging facility and provided us with meat. These people also took an interest in our emotional well-being. My youth pastor and leaders would call us to encourage us. My pastor's wife would pick me up for coffee. They helped us because their compassion moved them to action.

We were able to make it out of poverty because we had a tribe of people who showed us the love of Jesus by helping us with our practical needs. My mom would never have finished school without someone to help her with childcare. There were times that I could have been homeless if it hadn't been for people who found work for my mom to earn extra money. All the while, our friends and family would give us a ride to church. I didn't get saved until I was in middle school. But, I know that my life, had I not had the positive influence and prayers of the people at church, would have been much different. It was their prayers that gave rise to the voice inside of me urging me to walk away from situations that I shouldn't be in. There were many self-destructive things I did to myself, but it could have been so much worse. And, I had friends at church who modeled for me what it meant to be young but live a Christian life, while still having integrity and compassion for others. They genuinely cared for me. I will always be grateful for the hand the Lord had in my life and blessing me with these people.

My mom helped instill in me the value of getting an education. However, it wasn't until my late 20s that God blessed me by helping me get a job working for some really amazing women. These women pushed me to go back to school, encouraged me when I got frustrated, and mentored me. They believed in me, which is the most powerful thing they could have done for me. Knowing they believed I could achieve more was the strength and courage I needed to press on past the challenges I experienced while going to school, working, and raising a family. They taught me so much and I credit them for the success I have had in my career.

So, what can you do for people who are in a situation like I was in? In this chapter, I want to give you examples of what you can start thinking about to meet the needs of people in your church and eventually your local mission field. This is not an exhaustive list, simply a high-level overview of what you could start to think about. It is helpful to be knowledgeable of these various aspects of health and how they impact people, but at a local mission field level, God may only be calling you to meet one need. Also, remember, Rome wasn't built in a day and your outreach program won't be either! So, just start somewhere and start small. Later in this book, I will lay out practical steps to get you started.

Economic Stability: *Poverty, Employment, Food Insecurity, Housing Instability*

Poverty: You will start to notice that I will repeatedly refer you to first understand what is available within your own community. There are a lot of great nonprofits, community action agencies, and government programs available for people. Sometimes those who are in a financial crisis may not know how to navigate the system. Being that person to walk beside them may be all they need. You will be working with people who are going to be coming in and out of a financial crisis regularly. Another good place to start is to find ways to get money to help these people. Many people you will find fall into a gap; that place between poor enough to get assistance but still don't have enough to get by. Many people tend to not want to give financially to those in need for fear it isn't enough of a "hand up." However, I think that if someone is in financial need, giving them what they need is an opportunity to establish a relationship with them. Also, helping with a financial crisis decreases the chance they will accrue debt, which would further keep them from ever climbing out of that quintessential hole of poverty. Further, when compared to building the Kingdom, isn't it worth the investment? I love it when people come back to me multiple times because it gives me the opportunity to further build a relationship with them. So, when it is time to help give them that "hand up," they are receptive to listening to my advice about the next step to help them get out of that hole.

Employment: Get to know what is in your community in terms of employment agencies, trade schools, and colleges. Take time to go and meet with the directors of those agencies and learn about what programs they have available. Most of them have programs specifically targeting low-income people. Your role could simply be to facilitate connecting an individual to those programs. Look inwardly at your church as well. What type of people go to your church and what skills and knowledge do they have? In my church, I have people who are passionate about helping people create resumes and prepare for interviews. You could host workshops with that person leading it. You could also learn about the major industries in your community. Find out what their desired skills and employment process is. Then, help people navigate and get ready for that process. For example, if a community has a large factory industry, there may be math tests involved in employment and your church could consider a program to build math proficiency.

Food Insecurity: Food insecurity seems to be one of the most common symptoms of poverty. This is probably due to the fact that people end up spending their financial resources on things like housing and utilities and transportation. And, they probably can rely on the fact that food pantries and soup kitchens will be available to meet that need. So, as with many of the social determinants, the root cause of this issue is employment and economic stability. However, even though it is a symptom of a deeper problem, it is something that needs to be managed. For many churches, serving meals and starting pantries is a go to ministry. However, I want to encourage you to not just start another food pantry if one already exists in the neighborhood or near the neighborhood you are trying to reach. I would recommend only starting a new pantry if access to the one that exists is limited. So, what should you do instead? I would recommend that if your desire as a church is to meet food insecurity needs in the community you get behind an existing mechanism for addressing the need. Or, another approach might be just start a food co-op. The goal of helping people is not to just endlessly provide assistance, but to empower them to take ownership of their situation and to instill hope that there will be a day when their life will be different. There are faith-based food co-ops churches can implement that require members to pay 2 to 3 dollars each week to receive $50 worth of groceries, and this is done in partnership with your existing food bank. This model also empowers those who are participating and lets them hold onto their integrity. For many people living in poverty, asking for help can be accompanied with feelings of shame and guilt. Having a food co-op provides an opportunity for the overseeing church and members of the co-op to build relationships. Operations for the co-op are managed by the members so they learn ownership and responsibility versus becoming more dependent on other people.

Housing Instability: Housing instability is a difficult issue to tackle. There just isn't enough low-income housing for people who need it. This is because there are too many people who need it and also because it is costly to the state and city to maintain the housing that is available. However, churches can help people stay in their homes by offering support for rent, utilities, and even eviction relief. Because this can be costly, one requirement I have implemented is those requesting this assistance must have been denied by another method of support such as the Department of Health and Human Services. If you are a church who has more means, perhaps purchase an apartment building and implement a program that residents must go through to stay in the home such as a Bridges Out of Poverty or a church developed program.

Education: *High School Graduation, Enrollment in Higher Education, Language and Literacy*

Rather than going through each level of education, what we need to know is that increasing access to education is one of the best ways you can help people get out of poverty. The more education a person has, the more likely they are to take better care of themselves, their family, and get access to job opportunities, and there are many things we can do as a Church to address educational disparities. One thing to think about is asking people who are available during the day to mentor at-risk kids. We started a program a while ago in our church and it really requires very little effort: just one hour a week, per student, per mentor. Often, these kids do not have stability within their homes so having an adult who is attentive to them and willing to invest their time has a huge impact. Over the course of the years of us doing this mentorship program, the schools have commented on how the performance and behavior of the kids being mentored has improved.

But, a good place to start is to just go meet with the school principals and ask them exactly what they need. When I met with the school principal in our area, the three big things that she said they needed were books to send home to kids, hygiene products because those are not stocked typically at food pantries, and transportation for parents. So, we collected books and hosted a kids read day in the neighborhood where the lower income kids lived and did a hygiene drive at Christmas. As for transportation, churches could start a free ride volunteer service that runs throughout the day. Transportation is key not only for maintaining employment but the principal said that parents are unable to pick up sick children because they don't have a car to do so. Lack of transportation can also inhibit their ability to get to school.

Getting back to education, your church could start a scholarship fund for kids in the community. Another opportunity to support education is to offer tutoring and SAT/ACT prep. The possibilities are endless as to how we can support education in our communities.

Social Community Context: *Social Cohesion, Civic Participation, Perceptions of Discrimination and Equity, Incarceration*

Social Cohesion: Social cohesion is about knowing where you belong. Isn't this the very purpose behind why the author of Hebrews instructed us to not neglect meeting with one another (Hebrews 10:24-25)? People need people. We see in the very beginning that man was not created to be alone. God's plan was never for us to be isolated. In fact, His whole Church was created around the sense of being part of something bigger: a community, a body, a family. God doesn't want us to be in isolation. On all levels, He gives us the opportunity to be in a relationship with one another. We are born into a family, and then, He designed marriage for when we leave our family. There is also the blessing of the collective family of God. Not to mention that we are also in a relationship with God, Himself. It is this connectedness to Him and to each other that brings emotional well-being and stability. I believe that a contributing factor to poverty (and many other societal problems) is the weakened family unit. If healthy communities are built on healthy families, we should give individuals and families an opportunity to belong to a loving supportive environment. And, even better, we should find ways to celebrate diversity and include people from different backgrounds and cultures to be a part of our church families.

Civic Participation: Belonging to the family of God is such a gift. However, God did not intend for us to become a family so that we can only benefit from it. He also gave us ways to contribute to it. Paul touches on this in Romans 12:4-8, "For just as each of us has one body with many members, and these members do not all have the same function, so in Christ we, though many, form one body, and each member belongs to all the others. We have different gifts, according to the grace given to each of us. If your gift is prophesying, then prophesy in accordance with your faith; if it is serving, then serve; if it is teaching, then teach; if it is to encourage, then give encouragement; if it is giving, then give generously; if it is to lead, do it diligently; if it is to show mercy, do it cheerfully" (NIV). Helping others discover their strengths and how they can not only contribute to their community but the Kingdom of God, is the next step towards wholeness. This is where they gain confidence in the gifts that God has given them and begin to discover their purpose. Understanding one's purpose brings meaning to life, improves well-being, and helps with perspective during difficult times. Additionally, because of who we are, God's creation, we all have an innate desire (whether we are aware of it or not) to be a part of the plans of God. When we contribute we also develop a sense of ownership, which helps us gain control and power over our own lives. As a church leader, help people discover their strengths and invite them to participate in what you are doing in the community and in serving your own church body.

Perceptions of Discrimination and Equity: Discrimination and inequity can occur at many levels. The first level is structural, meaning policies and regulations that either intentionally or unintentionally are discriminatory such as residential segregation or access to education. Discrimination can also occur within an organization where policies and procedures or even unconscious biases cause inequity among employees such as one gender getting preferential treatment or promotions. There is also blatant discrimination at an individual level based on sex, gender, religion, and sexual identity.

This is a topic that I couldn't possibly do justice in just a couple paragraphs, but I will venture to say this: We need to be better. The Church has contributed to all of these forms of discrimination at one time or another and it is still apparent today. There are still people who belong to the KKK and claim to be Christian. There are also still "Christians" who treat women as being inferior. And, possibly the most relevant in these times, there are the hateful ways in which many Christians have engaged with the LGBTQ community. And, what is even worse, is that this is not occurring at an individual level, but it is condoned within church organizations.

While all forms of discrimination are wrong, I want to talk about discrimination against the LGBTQ community specifically because I don't think we talk about it enough. I know what the Bible says about homosexuality. I can't change the Bible and I trust in God's wisdom. But I also know that Jesus gave us two commandments: Love God and love people. Our job is to help others come into the right relationship with God through salvation and discipleship. Nowhere does the Bible say that we should go around telling people they need to fix sin in their lives before God will accept them. The whole point of the Gospel is that we are all sinners and fall short of the glory of God (Romans 3:23). Ephesians 2:8-9 says, "For by grace you have been saved through faith. And this is not your own doing; it is the gift of God, not a result of works, so that no one may boast" (ESV). There is too much self-righteousness in the Church. Many of us need to stop judging and start loving. Judgement is the terminal illness of the Church. If you want to know why the Church is dying, that's it. Did you know that it is not uncommon for those who identify as LGBTQ and Christian to also be ostracized from the LGBTQ community? So where do they get to belong? Forty percent of homeless youth identify as LGBTQ, as many are homeless because they are rejected from their families and asked to leave their homes. Further, many who identify as LGBTQ are aware of what Scripture says about homosexuality. There is no need to rub salt in the wound, so to speak. I have a friend who is a lesbian. She has been told her entire life that she is an abomination and that she will go to Hell. She was told that God hates her. So many times I have spoken to her about the love of God, but she is terrified to accept salvation because she believes God hates her. I don't think that this experience is unique to my friend. God hates sin, not people. This is why we all need Jesus. We have to ask God to soften our hearts to teach us how to love the LGBTQ community. Each of them are precious to God as we are. God wants every single person no matter what their sin is to be a part of His family. All I know is that there is no condemnation for those who are in Christ (Romans 8:1) and that only the Holy Spirit convicts of sin (John 16:8). Therefore, since none of us can earn our salvation, why do we ostracize this single sin? We are all guilty; that is the point. I encourage each of us to do what Jesus said in Matthew 9:13, "Go and learn what this means: 'I desire mercy, not sacrifice.' For I have not come to call the righteous, but sinners" (NIV).

So, what can we do as a Church to address discrimination in our communities? First, is to reflect on what biases we have in our own hearts and ask God what to do about them. We have no idea the struggles or contributing factors as to why people behave the way they do because we have never walked in their shoes. So, we can choose mercy over judgement and allow God to address their hearts. Second, be the voice for those who can't speak for themselves (Proverbs 31:8-9). We can't sit silently on the sidelines and do nothing while racism runs rampant in our communities. Silence and turning the other way is just as bad as being the perpetrator. Thirdly, recognize that because of race, gender, sexuality, or socioeconomic status, you have access to different opportunities that others who are different from you might not have. Look for ways to help those who have barriers to opportunities. Lastly, be intentional about meeting and being friends with people who are not like you. How will you learn if you keep yourself around only what is familiar to you? Galatians 3:28 says, "There is neither Jew nor Gentile, neither slave nor free, nor is there male and female, for you are all one in Christ

Jesus" (NIV). If God sees us all as equal in Christ, shouldn't we want to reflect that in how we view one another?

Incarceration: According to HealthyPeople.gov, "In 2014, there were approximately 2.2 million people incarcerated in state or federal prisons and local jails, and an additional 4.7 million individuals under community supervision (i.e., on probation or parole)." People who are incarcerated or have been incarcerated are at a higher risk for chronic disease and mental health issues. Further, many who are incarcerated have a history of neglect or abuse. There are many things the Church can do to help this population of people. You could volunteer to teach classes in the prison, hold services, offer inner healing sessions, or start a mentorship program by partnering with jails and prisons in your area. There are also many needs that we may not think about occurring within our prison system such as female inmates entering into prison while pregnant or inmates who are aging. Additionally, churches could commit to finding families within our churches to adopt children from their local adoption agencies where their babies would be sent.

Moreover, challenges don't only exist for those who are currently in prison, but often for those who are no longer in prison. People who serve their sentence often lack familial connections and find it difficult to find jobs. The Church could help by creating opportunities for these former inmates to gain life and work skills while establishing a work history. For example, friends of mine have opened a coffee shop where they exclusively hire former inmates. Churches could also help by having men and women in their church mentor inmates as they transition to their new lives. Business owners could also make a commitment to hire those who have had a criminal past.

Health and Healthcare: Giving people access to healthcare may seem like the most daunting of all the social determinants, and in some ways it is. With the increasing costs of healthcare delivery in healthcare reform and rising costs of insurance premiums, it seems like a situation out of our control. However, there are things that churches can do to address this. You could partner with your local community health department to host free clinics for things like vaccinations and dental care. You could also work with your local hospital to develop community health workers who would be volunteers from your church; these are people who are trained to advocate for those who cannot advocate for themselves within the health systems. They also can provide education post peer support groups or be home aides that are free for those who cannot afford or do not have eligibility for such benefits. I have also heard of churches purchasing medical bill debt to decrease debt for those living in their area.

Neighborhood and Built Environment *Access to Healthy Foods, Quality of Housing, Crime and Violence, Environmental Conditions*

Access to Healthy Foods: There are many ways your church can increase access to healthy food. We discussed a couple options earlier in this chapter. Starting things like food co-ops is a great way to ensure that people in your local mission field have access to food. But that might not be feasible and you may want to be supportive of your local food pantry. Your church could provide volunteers to help that church pantry keep going. Or, you could host fundraising events to help raise money for replenishing the food pantry. Additionally, you could start a community garden. A community garden not only increases access to healthy foods, it helps to grow a sense of community within the neighborhood. Perhaps in addition to the community garden, you could host cooking events to teach people about food and how to prepare fresh fruits and vegetables.

Quality of Housing: I remember watching a documentary about children living in an inner-city area. The houses that they lived in we're old and dusty and had mold. There was a high incidence of asthma in small children living in the area. This asthma caused kids to have attacks that were so severe they ended up in the emergency room more than once in a single month. So, a community group got a grant to rebuild the neighborhood. They built new houses and installed air filtration systems. They also included things like a library and community center, and installing sidewalks so that people could go for walks. Once the families moved into the new homes, they saw not only a decrease but an elimination of asthma related emergency room visits. This is significant because it was a way of meeting a practical need that decreased the overutilization of resources in the healthcare system, but it also greatly impacted the quality of life for the families. Every church may not have the ability to obtain a grant and rebuild a neighborhood; however, you could have a ministry that builds handicap ramps, does practical projects like repairs roofs or raises money for new water heaters and furnaces, or a radical ministry might be raising money to help families with down payments for homes. With rent as high as it is, many families could afford a mortgage payment, however it's the upfront cash needed for down payment and closing costs that tend to present trouble for them.

Crime and Violence: The best way to address crime and violence in neighborhoods is to prevent it from happening in the first place by providing opportunities for children and families to come together. To start, as a church leader, take some time to go to your police department's website. Most of them participate in reporting that allows you to see not only where crime is happening in your community, but what type of crime. Use this data to understand what is happening and then identify an intervention for addressing it. For example, if you have a lot of domestic abuse occurring, find ways to work with your police department so that you can help restore those families. If there is a lot of drug abuse, there are many levels of intervention. The first is prevention by educating the community, particularly children and youth. The next level of intervention is working with college students to prevent or offer help with addiction. Lastly, partner with recovery houses and organizations and support the work they are doing to help people live sober lives.

Environmental Conditions: Environmental conditions can have an impact on a person's health. This can be related to pollution, mold in homes, provisions for homes of the disabled, safe neighborhoods, and having access to safe places for children and families to spend time. Home repairs and helping those who are disabled with modifications for their homes to make them accessible is an easy place to start for churches. These modifications are typically not covered by insurance and are costly to install. And, while some funding is available through governmental assistance programs, it doesn't cover the entire cost and often isn't available to those who are above the poverty line, but do not have enough to pay for such enhancements to their homes such as with the elderly. However, I would suggest churches take some time to drive around their community, look at the state of the houses, and work at understanding what is happening in your area. Particularly that of where your church is located. Use your church building as a safe place for families. You can offer reading programs, parenting classes, game nights, etc., and even offer a meal to families when they are there.

Church, we are called to be a city on the hill and to be all things to all people (Matt. 5:14; 1 Cor. 9:19-23). We, as the Church, need to accept the responsibility that we are to care for the poor and downtrodden and not leave it up to non-profits and governmental programs. Addressing social determinants and the practical needs within our communities is necessary, but is not a means to an end. Meeting practical needs should be viewed as a mechanism or a way to create opportunities to build relationships with the people we are helping. This understanding is the pivotal difference between traditional assistance programs and the Church. The real, lasting remedy to these needs is helping those individuals improve their quality of life by enabling them to become whole through a relationship with God. It is only Jesus who can truly transform lives, so we must help them be dependent on Him and not us--because we are not their savior. However, when we talk about being the light in the darkness, establishing programs such as these brings light to communities that otherwise might be desperate and hopeless. Eradicating poverty is an impossible dream, but with God all things are possible. If we all do our part to build the Kingdom by addressing poverty in our cities, we can make lasting changes.

Reflection

Think through your life and the social determinants of health. What experiences have you had related to them? How did God provide a way for you to overcome these challenges?

Prayer

Holy Spirit, thank you that you speak to me and are the revealer of truth. Open my eyes to the things in my community that need attention. Show me the pain and suffering occurring in front of me. Give me wisdom to know who you want me to help and how to do it. In Jesus Name, Amen.

Chapter 8

"Ask me and I will tell you remarkable secrets you do not know about things to come."
—Jeremiah 33:3

After reading the last chapter, you may be feeling overwhelmed by all the things communities need in order to be healthy and live life in abundance. It is overwhelming to think about all the dysfunction within our cities and the impact it has on our society. However, it is not your responsibility to save your city by yourself. That is for the Church. If every church could work on just one slice of the pie, then all needs would be taken care of. This means each church has to define what piece of the pie is for them, but, luckily, you don't have to manage that part by yourself either.

Each pastor and church leader needs to understand what their *metron* (Strong, G3358) is for their church. A metron, in the Greek, literally means a measure or limit. Each church has a metron they are responsible for. Paul refers to this in 2 Corinthians 10:13, "We, however, will not boast beyond proper limits, but will confine our boasting to the sphere of service God Himself has assigned to us, a sphere that also includes you" (NIV). Paul is telling the Corinthians they are within his sphere of responsibility. So it should also be for each individual church. There is a divine assignment for you in your geographical area. For some churches, this sphere might be small to start. However, your level of responsibility and influence should grow. If you do not see God building your network and ability to serve more in your community, then I encourage you to ask Him why that is.

When I think of mentrons, I picture a bullseye. In the middle of the bullseye are your people in your individual church. This center circle is all about making sure the needs of the people within your individual church are being met. These needs could be anything related to spiritual growth to practical needs. The next ring on the bullseye represents the neighbors of the church. These are the people, families, and businesses that are geographically near your church. Moving to the next sphere, or metron, means building relationships with those businesses and developing ways to connect with the people who live near the church. This should not mean they get a mailed invitation to a special event several times a year, but instead the church is actively engaging in serving those neighbors in some capacity. In order to move to this next ring, you need to understand what the needs are. No matter where your church is located, whether it be a wealthy neighborhood or poor neighborhood, there are needs to be met. For example, children of wealthy families could experience isolation if both parents have demanding work schedules. Or, there may be wives who don't work outside of the home who may need fellowship with other women. The point is you need to know the people who your church is responsible for. The next sphere of the bullseye is your city, then your region or state, then national, and then international. How you progress from one sphere to the next is something God has a strategy for that you can access.

Many churches do a great job of staying connected with those within their congregation. However, this seems to be where many churches get stuck. Or, they might say they are involved in missions because they are sending money to support an international ministry or even a local ministry or non-profit. Yet, many churches lack the understanding as to how local missions should pertain to improving the health (or wholeness) of their own community. Not to say that local missions are better than international missions or vice versa. I don't think it is a question of either or; I think it is more about being purposeful in finding balance between all of it, but more importantly asking God what it is He wants you to do with the resources He has given you. Just as Jesus instructed the disciples in Acts 1:8, "Rather, you will receive power when the Holy Spirit has come upon you, and you will be my witnesses in Jerusalem, in all Judea and Samaria, and to the end of the earth" (CEB); we should look to start in our "Jerusalem" first before going to "Samaria and to the end of the earth."

However, first and foremost, we should not skip over the first part of this verse- the part about the Holy Spirit. Jesus told the apostles to wait for the Holy Spirit before they could continue His ministry. There is a deception existing within the Church that says the Holy Spirit is dormant and not active today. There is also a false belief that He is scary and somehow not part of the Godhead. Some Christians, in a nutshell, view Him as some crazy cousin we acknowledge, but don't really include as being part of the family. This falsehood has to change if we are going to transform cities because if the first witnesses needed the Holy Spirit to share the Gospel, then so do we. Not acknowledging our need for the Holy Spirit insinuates we can build His Church on our own, with our own strength, without His help. We are the same Church, or are supposed to be the same Church, as in the first Church in the Book of Acts. It was the Holy Spirit that emboldened the Apostles to preach the Gospel and told them where to go next. It is this same connection and dependence on the Holy Spirit that is needed in our Church today. If Jesus is our ultimate example, remember that even He only did what the Father told Him (John 5:19). The way we hear from the Father is through the Holy Spirit. If we continue to exclude Him from the equation, the Church will continue to do good things but not God things. What I mean is, our typical paradigm in the Church, whether individually or as a church organization, is to decide on good things to do and then ask God to bless them. Rather, we should be asking God, what it is He wants to accomplish and then trust Him to provide the means necessary to make it happen.

In order to mobilize your church, you need to help your people learn how to minister in a way that is in step with the Holy Spirit. Listening and responding to His voice is the catalyst for transforming people and cities. You can have soup kitchens and women's ministries, but if people aren't encountering God through your ministry, then that should be a point of concern. For example, you could hold a mobile food pantry and feed hundreds of families. That is a good thing. But, you could hold that same mobile food pantry event and have your people ministering to people in the cars by praying with them for healing or peace in their circumstances. They could be getting to know them and making a connection with them on a personal level. That is doing ministry the way that Jesus did ministry. The best place to start to help people connect with the Holy Spirit is to demystify what people think about Him and educate them with the truth. Simply, make it a safe place for people to encounter God through the Holy Spirit.

If you were raised in a denomination that does not believe in the workings of the Holy Spirit today, I encourage you to study the scriptures that reference Him again and ask Him what it is He wants you to know about who He is and the role He wants in your life and ministry. Oftentimes, we make knowing Him out to be something more than it is. And, truth be told, there has been a lot of misuse and misinformation about the Holy Spirit in churches over the years. But knowing the Holy Spirit is as simple as asking Him to reveal Himself to you. My daughter, who was 8 years old at this time, was reading the book of Ephesians. She set a task for herself to write down everything that book said about her identity in Christ. She eventually made her way to this verse: "and to know this love that surpasses knowledge—that you may be filled to the measure of all the fullness of God" (Eph 3:19, NIV). She came down from her room and showed me the scripture and simply said, "Mom, I want that. How do I get filled with the fullness of God?" We prayed at that moment that the Holy Spirit would fill her. Since then, I have seen a noticeable shift in her countenance and her fervor to know more of God and study His Word. While I am glad I got to pray with her, I don't believe it was my prayer that made the difference; rather, it was her simple declaration, "I want that," and her willingness to accept the gifts God has for her. That is all it takes to be filled with the fullness of God. You just have to decide you want it and submit to being open to whatever His fullness looks like because there is nothing to fear.

To help the people in your church engage with the Holy Spirit, it has to start at the very center of the bullseye that I mentioned early. You are the dead center of the bullseye; you are your first metron. In order to know your metron, you must allow yourself to be open to His guidance by walking in step with the Spirit (Galatians 5:16). So, to hear God and thereby walk in step with the Spirit, you need to:

Recognize that you are one with God. Jesus prayed in John 17:20-21, "I pray not only for these, but also for those who will trust in me because of their word, 21 that they may all be one. Just as you, Father, are united with me and I with you, I pray that they may be united with us, so that the world may believe that you sent me" (CJB). There is no separation between us and God whatsoever.

Believe the Holy Spirit lives in you. We need the Holy Spirit just as the apostles did and Jesus promised that He would send the Holy Spirit (John 14:26). Paul asks in 1 Corinthians 6:19-20, "Do you not know that your bodies are temples of the Holy Spirit, who is in you, whom you have received from God? You are not your own; you were bought at a price" (NIV). Or, in Romans 5:5, "And hope does not put us to shame, because God's love has been poured out into our hearts through the Holy Spirit, who has been given to us." We are the temple of the Holy Spirit and its presence in us is the source of love that we are to give to others.

Get out of agreement with the lie that you can't hear from God. Any thought that doesn't align with God's Word is a lie. God's Word says that not only can you hear His voice, but that He promises to tell you things you couldn't have possibly known (Jer. 33:3; John 10:27-30).

Practice hearing from God. Get a journal and just start asking God questions. Write down exactly word for word what comes to your mind. Don't worry about synthesizing what all the words mean or where the thought is going, just write one word at a time. Or, sometimes God speaks in pictures, so draw or describe the picture you see.

Stop questioning if it is your voice or God's voice. This questioning is based in fear that we can't hear from God or that we aren't capable of telling the difference between His voice and ours. It paralyzes us and keeps us from moving or acting when the Spirit is asking us to. As long as we know the Word of God and what we are hearing is in line with that, if we get it wrong, there is grace.

Develop a habit of listening and responding. In John 5:19, Jesus says, "Very truly I tell you, the Son can do nothing by himself; he can do only what he sees his Father doing, because whatever the Father does the Son also does." If we are to live by the example of Jesus, shouldn't we develop this discipline of listening and responding to what the Father is doing?

Walking in step with the Spirit is about first transforming your mind and believing that you can. However, I will say that for me, journaling has been one of my most powerful tools. Writing it down helps you slow down and really listen and be dependent on hearing the Holy Spirit. The most important part is to not judge what you have written. If it aligns with God's Word, there is no reason to second guess it. Often, I look back at my journal and am encouraged by the things God has spoken to me. It helps me remember prayers that He has answered, and made me feel more confident in my faith and ability to hear Him because I have seen the things God spoke to me become reality. Furthermore, talking to God doesn't mean it has to happen at a major life event: it can be as simple as having a conversation.

There are times I have said, "Lord, I don't know where my keys are. Can you help me?" And, He tells me exactly where to go. Now, also happening in that situation is me trying to remember where I left them and if my kids had taken them. Then, likely, I am running late which means my blood pressure is starting to rise because I can't find my keys. But, when I pause and just ask God for His help, He tells me exactly what to do. I am getting to the point where I am completely dependent on hearing His voice before acting. But, admittedly, I am not perfect at it. I know I am not doing it when I experience frustration and strife. Just like when I lose my keys, I try to figure it out on my own, but peace and resolution come when I seek Him first. This is the level of dependence we should have on God: we can do nothing without Him first telling us to do it. We also need to help others have this dependence. This is particularly important for those we help who are living in poverty. We want to be sure we are pushing them towards dependence on Jesus and not towards dependence on us. Once you get confident in hearing Him in your quiet times, you will become more aware of the voice of the Holy Spirit when you are doing ministry.

In order to allow the Holy Spirit to guide you during ministry, you have to be willing to be a fool. Oftentimes people are afraid to act on what they hear from the Holy Spirit because they will be embarrassed if they are wrong. Loving and encouraging others is never wrong. And, the more that you put yourself out there by being obedient to the Spirit, the easier it will become to know what to do. Honestly, only twice has someone refused prayer or ministry when I have felt led to talk to them. So, give yourself a chance to practice. It is also helpful to spend time listening to God before you engage in ministry activities because you can ask Him to show you ahead of time who you should minister to. You can do this by writing in your journal what God reveals and shows you. John 5:19-20 tells us that Jesus said, "Truly, truly, I say to you, the Son can do nothing of His own accord, but only what He sees the Father doing. For whatever the Father does, that the Son does likewise. For the Father loves the Son and shows Him all that He Himself is doing. And greater works than these will He show Him, so that you may marvel" (NLT). Jesus was so connected to the Father that when He moved, Jesus moved. Is that not also how we should approach our ministry? Think about that for a moment: Jesus could do *nothing* without the Father telling Him to do it. When we become believers, we have access to this knowledge. In fact, Scripture says, we have the very mind of Christ (1 Corinthians 2:16). This entirely new perspective exceeds all earthly knowledge and wisdom because we are one with Christ.

It is our union in Christ that should inform our every thought and action. Yet, instead, it is common to see Christians strive to make things happen on their own. We use our own knowledge to decide what to do instead of asking Jesus to guide us. Jesus is our very lifeline, just as He described in the parable of the branches and vines (John 15:1-17). In that parable, Jesus described what a relationship with Him is like. When looking at a vine, we do not think the branches are distinct from the vine itself. In fact, they are extensions of the vine on which the vine grows its fruit. We are to be connected to Him because apart from Him there is no life. We are also meant to be that extension to the world bearing the fruit of the Holy Spirit (Gal. 5:22-23). Without the vine, the branches can't grow. It is the vine that carries all sustenance needed for the branches. In fact, the branches cannot exist without the vine because it is from the vine that they grow in the first place. What does this mean practically? This means that we have to be in unity with Jesus so that we don't see ourselves apart from Him in any way. The Bible says to put on Christ like new clothes. We like to think about Jesus as living in our heart, but that's not accurate. When we become believers and followers of Jesus, it is a complete immersion into Him. He fills us with the Holy Spirit, making us holy temples and then He surrounds us with His love and grace. There is no separation from Him at all. He is in us and we are in Him (1 John 4:13).

We can live in confidence that we are immersed in Jesus who is immersed in the Father. And just as John 17:22-26 describes, "The glory that you have given me I have given to them, that they may be one even as we are one, I in them and you in me, that they may become perfectly one, so that the world may know that you sent me and loved them even as you loved me. Father, I desire that they also, whom you have given me, may be with me where I am, to see my glory that you have given me because you loved me before the foundation of the world. O righteous Father, even though the world does not know you, I know you, and these know that you have sent me. I made known to them your name, and I will continue to make it known, that the love with which you have loved me may be in them, and I in them" (ESV). Jesus prayed that we would be one with God just as He is. However, the application of this unity takes some practice. The most fundamental step is to get the revelation that you are one with Christ. Then, it means that we have to be intentional about pausing and asking God, Jesus, and the Holy Spirit: What should I be thinking right now? What is my next step? How should I handle this situation? And because we are attached to that lifeline, we have direct access to that knowledge just as Jesus did.

Another travesty wreaking havoc in the Church today is the loss of identity. If we really understand and know who we are in Christ, our entire world looks differently. We are also supposed to walk in power and authority over things on Earth. When Jesus ascended the mountain, He said, "Very truly I tell you, whoever believes in me will do the works I have been doing, and they will do even greater things than these, because I am going to the Father. And I will do whatever you ask in my name, so that the Father may be glorified in the Son. You may ask me for anything in my name, and I will do it" (John 14: 12-14, NIV). Let that sink in for a moment. He said *anyone who believes in him* would do greater things than He did? That means it isn't just special people who hold offices in the Church who get to do the same things Jesus did. Jesus raised people from the dead! It means every single believer can do what He did because of the power of the Holy Spirit. Knowing this should impact the way we pray so that we aren't doing it halfheartedly, but instead with power and authority. Jesus has empowered us through the Holy Spirit to have dominion over these things on Earth. If we lived like this, there is nothing that we couldn't do (Luke 17:6). This is particularly important when we talk about caring for the poor. It takes vast resources to do this work, but we are the children of God and citizens of Heaven. This means that we have access to all those resources. One of the things God has taught me as I have built my own outreach initiatives is how limitless the supply of Heaven is. Any time that I have needed anything, despite my momentary lapses of faith, God has delivered exactly what I needed when I needed it. For example, I wanted to purchase a truckload of food to feed hungry families. I don't know if it was something that God had asked me to do or just a desire that I had within my heart, but I didn't have enough money in my budget to purchase it. I was disappointed because I knew what a difference it would make in the community, but I trusted that God would provide if it was supposed to happen. A couple weeks before Thanksgiving, a friend of mine who knew nothing about my desire to purchase this truck of food called me. He said that he wanted to purchase a truck of food and asked if my local mission field could use it. This is just one example of the many ways that God has sent resources to me when it was needed: it is always in His perfect timing. Another time I needed to purchase a new furnace for a family. Their furnace went out on a day that the weather was so cold there was an advisory to not go outside. The severe weather meant that furnaces were running nonstop. It would cost $3,000 to replace the furnace for that family. I had no idea how I was going to get that money, but I knew that I needed to. So, I asked the Lord who I should call and began making phone calls. Within two hours, I had the $3,000 and within another two hours that family had a new furnace. I am so grateful for how God provides and I never want to have a sense of entitlement. But the truth is that our Father loves us and enjoys blessing us and He certainly provides according to His will. And, isn't His will always to take care of His children and express His love to people? To transform cities, you have to be comfortable with the kind of faith in God to do such amazing things, that people think you are a little crazy.

So, to mobilize your church to transform cities, these are the values that need to be in place and modeled by the leadership in your church: embracing the Holy Spirit, listening to His voice, being one with Jesus, and having faith in God to do the miraculous. There were times I was frustrated because I went to a church that did not value these things. And, since I wasn't the pastor of the Church, all I could do was model it in my own life and pray for God to shift things for my church. While I could have left to find a church that did value these things, I stayed because I felt like that church was my metron. God had placed me there for a specific purpose to do what He wanted me to do, and not what I was getting out of going to church there. So, if that is you, I want to encourage you to stay the course and rely on Him to do the work. If there is anything to be learned from our unity in Christ, it is our access to supernatural rest-- remember, nothing about this plan is your responsibility. You are only called to be obedient to the things God asks you to do, just like Jesus. We experience God's rest when we allow ourselves to be led by His Spirit, fully trust Him, and are in complete submission to His will. The only responsibility you have is to remain in unity with Jesus and obedient to what you are being asked to do. The moment you begin trying to make this happen on your own is the moment the ministry shifts from Him to you (Hebrews 4:11).

Reflection

Read John 16:13. Read the verse in several translations. My favorite version is in The Passion Translation.

Take some time to sit and listen to the Holy Spirit. Focus on the truth in this verse. Read it several times. What does the Holy Spirit want to reveal to you about your metron? The metron of your church? Journal about what He reveals to you.

Prayer

Holy Spirit, thank you for revealing the truth to me. Thank you that I do not have any responsibility for saving my city. In fact, right now, I release any false sense of responsibility I may have for making this happen to you, Jesus. Thank you that your burden is light. Today, I commit to following only your lead. I also declare that I can hear your voice clearly. I ask you to open my eyes and ears so that I see your work and hear what you want me to do next. In Jesus Name, Amen.

Chapter 9

"Spiritual life flows out of union with Christ, not merely imitation of Christ."

– Richard F. Lovelace

I have said throughout this book that the ultimate goal isn't to only invest in addressing social determinants of health because, truth be told, those are only band aids on a much bigger problem. Ultimately, we want people to experience wholeness in every aspect of their lives. However, we know that we can't just address wholeness, because the crisis warrants immediate action and that is where addressing the social determinants of health comes in. Through establishing relationships with people, we get invited into their lives and are able to help them through a process towards wholeness which addresses the deeper issues. When you are in a relationship with someone, that is when you can actually help them walk with Jesus to heal the broken areas of their life. In order to reach people in poverty, we have to let go of our preconceived notions and judgements around the fact that they are poor and instead view them with compassion and empathize with the strife they endure on a daily basis.

Something that has been lost in the modern church is equipping believers with how to share their faith. When I grew up, the way in which we communicate our faith was focused on sharing Gospel tracks and diagrams of two cliffs and the cross bridging the gap between them. But, sharing the Gospel shouldn't be that elaborate or complicated. You shouldn't have to memorize a bunch of verses or illustrations. Rather, sharing the love of Christ should be an overflow from what we are experiencing within ourselves. If we are not experiencing God on a daily basis, that should be cause for concern. People are in desperate need of love. Each of us has an inherent need to be loved, accepted, and fully known or understood. Who else can do that but God? Conversely, we cannot talk about salvation without the acknowledgment of God's judgment. It seems like this is something we shy away from. There is a fear in the Church to speak up about the things that are counter to God's Word, and we have a fear of offending people because we have been conditioned to believe that love is allowing someone to live however they want to live. But, in actuality, love is speaking the truth. Romans 12:2 says, "Do not conform to the pattern of this world, but be transformed by the renewing of your mind. Then you will be able to test and approve what God's will is—His good, pleasing and perfect will" (NIV). However, I fear that as a Church, it has become harder and harder to see the line that is drawn between God's Word and what our culture says is acceptable. It is only going to get worse, which is why we need to be vigilant in knowing God's Word. The truth is, God's judgment is very real and those who do not follow Jesus will not be saved when they die or when judgment comes. Ezekiel 33:4-6 says, "'Then if anyone hears the trumpet but does not heed the warning and the sword comes and takes their life, their blood will be on their own head. Since they heard the sound of the trumpet but did not heed the warning, their blood will be on their own head. If they had heeded the warning, they would have saved themselves. But if the watchman sees the sword coming and does not blow the trumpet to warn the people and the sword comes and takes someone's life, that person's life will be taken because of their sin, but I will hold the watchman accountable for their blood'" (NIV). We are the watchmen who know this judgement is coming, yet we are not sounding the warning bell. Our job as leaders in the Church is to equip the saints to build up the Body of Christ and to fulfill the great commission to go and make disciples of all nations (Matt. 28:16-20). If our people do not know how to share their faith, how can we expect to mobilize our churches to truly transform their cities?

In modern church culture, we have seen a shift in which many people are excited about their church and are able to tell their friends about their amazing church, but spend less time boasting about their amazing savior. Reasons this might occur include simply they lack the spiritual maturity to do so, but more likely they aren't equipped to do so. Once a person accepts Christ, discipleship often focuses on reading the Bible and knowing the scriptures and less on activating them as Kingdom-builders. True and complete wholeness can only be achieved through experiencing Jesus. This is why it is imperative we activate the Church to be spirit led so we all can proclaim the Gospel confidently and boldly. It is through experiencing the love and redemption that comes through salvation this wholeness is possible.

There are often two things that prevent people from truly experiencing wholeness in their lives: they don't have a good relationship or understanding of the Father or they don't know their identity in Christ. Spiritual wholeness is pivotal because until these two broken relationships, the one with God and the one with ourselves, are healed it will be a struggle to gain true wholeness in any other aspect of our lives.

For example, if a person believes God does not love them, it will be hard for them to understand that God wants good things for them. Or, if they believe God's character is to punish, it will be difficult for them to believe that God is patient, kind, and generous. Further, if they don't know their true identity in Christ, they will never understand their purpose or what they are truly capable of. This means they may miss out on the abundance they can experience when all 7 Pillars of Wholeness are addressed:

The Spiritual Pillar - Refers to your spiritual health and wholeness, addressing things like your relationship with God and your identity in Christ.

The Mental Pillar - Refers to your intellectual and mental health, addressing things pertaining to your ways of thinking and need for mind renewal.

The Emotional Pillar - Refers to your emotional health, addressing things like your character and emotional maturity.

The Relational Pillar - Refers to the health of your relationships, addressing things like your ability to set boundaries, resolve conflicts, and develop and sustain healthy relationships.

The Financial Pillar - Refers to your financial IQ, addressing the ways that you think about money and how to best invest, save, give away, and spend your money.

The Physical Pillar - Refers to your physical health and wholeness, addressing things like divine healing and taking good care of your physical body.

The Vocational Pillar - Refers to your calling in life, addressing things like your career, your earning potential, your life purpose, and how you use your gifts to serve humanity.

Some may be able to achieve a measure of wholeness relating to the pillars; nevertheless, without understanding their intimacy with God, and thereby their true identity, it will be achieved through struggle and strife because it will be done independent of God, instead of in union with God, and therefore it will never be complete.

In some ways, the Church contributes to some of these misconceptions about God and who we are because we view His Word through our own personal lens. And, in the same way that those we help may have a broken idea of who God is or who they are, so do we—and therefore, we communicate what God says through that filter. We also promote spiritual wholeness as being achieved through performance by focusing on what we or others need to do in order for God to be pleased with us. Despite what Paul tells us in Ephesians 2:3-10, "All of us also lived among them at one time, gratifying the cravings of our flesh and following its desires and thoughts. Like the rest, we were by nature deserving of wrath. But because of His great love for us, God, who is rich in mercy, made us alive with Christ even when we were dead in transgressions—it is by grace you have been saved. And God raised us up with Christ and seated us with Him in the heavenly realms in Christ Jesus, in order that in the coming ages He might show the incomparable riches of His grace, expressed in His kindness to us in Christ Jesus. For it is by grace you have been saved, through faith—and this is not from yourselves, it is the gift of God— not by works, so that no one can boast. For we are God's handiwork, created in Christ Jesus to do good works, which God prepared in advance for us to do" (NIV). We focus on the transgressions and the sin. We talk about whether we are doing enough to nurture our relationship with God, and in doing so there is this constant fear of "backsliding" that many Christians live in bondage to every day. Focusing on our sin and our Christian performance makes our salvation about us and not about Jesus. Yes, to be saved, we not only have to believe Jesus is the Son of God, we also must believe Jesus is our Lord, which means that in all things, we follow His example that He set for us while devoting our lives to the work He has prepared for us to do. Living an authentic life founded on the truths of God is not focusing on our sin, but instead focusing on the truth that has been revealed through Jesus and the Holy Spirit: you are saved, forgiven, redeemed, and empowered. At some point, we have to help people move away from their identity as a sinner, so they can face their new life as a new creation living in union with Jesus and all the inheritance that it comes with—wholeness.

In the book, Helping People to Change, Richard Boyatizis, Melvin Smith, and Ellen Van Oosten compile their research on how to help people change. One way that doesn't work is what they call "coaching for compliance." This is when we use an external goal or task we are focused on in order to motivate someone to change. In the Church, this looks like reading your Bible or praying for a certain number of hours or minutes per day or tithing a certain amount of money. When these external goals are not met, it perpetuates feelings of failure, guilt, and even shame. This also looks like a person who is living in poverty and we focus on telling them to create a budget or get a better job. Focusing on achieving this external goal doesn't help the person fix the intrinsic motivation. Instead, the authors show in their research that real, lasting change only happens when we "coach with compassion." We coach others with compassion when we are genuinely concerned for the person's well-being and are focused on them.

The authors go on to say that coaching with compassion is done when the coach or mentor helps the person discover their true selves. This is rooted in their hopes, dreams, and passions and who they think themselves to be. The authors also suggest identifying any blind spots the person may have by getting feedback from others, so that they get a holistic view of who they are. I agree with this approach, but would push us to go deeper. A person's true self shouldn't be validated by what others think of them (Gal. 1:10), but only in what God thinks of them. Further, who a person is intrinsically is only who God created them to be, therefore our true identity can only be found in Him. Our identity is only found in Him because there is no separation between us and Him. It is only through this revelation of complete union with Christ that people can discover who they truly are. In his pamphlet, "No Independent Self," Norman Grubbs describes the human being as a container that can be filled with darkness (the flesh or sinful nature) or with light (Holy Spirit). He says, "The Spirit gives inner witness of the replacement of the Spirit of Truth for that false spirit of error. This is the radical revelation to those who cannot stop short of our total inheritance." It is this very revelation that shifts our perspective from what we can do to achieve wholeness (inheritance) from performance based on our own abilities rather than that of

Christ. This is the arc that Paul describes in his letter to the Romans. He talks about the power of sin is only there when we are bound to the Law. But, in Christ, we are no longer bound to the law because we died with Christ, therefore breaking the hold that the Law has on us. Instead, we are propelled into this new way of living by the Spirit. When the Spirit lives in us, it changes us from the inside out. We begin to express His very nature rather than our own. Grubbs also makes the argument that both darkness and light cannot exist within the same vessel, so the new creation is in the filling up of light within us. In other words, the fruit we bear isn't based on the branch (us), it is determined by the vine that we are connected to (spirit or flesh). It is impossible for a branch to bear two kinds of fruit. Therefore, a person cannot know their true identity if they continue to believe that they are made separate from Him. The believer's reality is that we are not separate, but one with Him and in Him (John 17:21-23). Grubbs says, "I accept and recognize the reality of these flesh pulls, but I am dead to them in Christ ('always bearing about in the body the dying of the Lord Jesus' as in Corinthians 4:10). They can shout at me by temptation, but have no hold or right to me (Rom. 8:12). I am alive unto God, a Spirit person and led by the Spirit. The only law on me is what I know to instinctively fulfill, that 'Law of the Spirit' by which I spontaneously do the things of the Spirit. Through Christ, the Spirit has replaced that old 'Law of sin and death' by which I spontaneously did the things of the flesh. So I go free—back to who I really always was." It is understanding this pivotal difference between the old self and the new creation that brings freedom to people because "where the spirit of the Lord is, there is freedom" (2 Corinth 3:17, NIV). This is vastly different than what we have been taught in regards to how to deal with sinful "pulls." Instead we have allowed believers to continue to be slaves to sin by coaching with compliance and focusing on turning away from sin on their own.

However, God coaches us with compassion. He reveals to us our true selves, and stretches us to who He has made us to be by getting us to shift our perspective from the here and now to what He has called us to do. He told Abram and Sarai that they would be father and mother to nations even though they were elderly, without children, and Sarai was barren. The change he made in them was so great, He changed their names from Abram to Abraham and Sarai to Sarah. To Moses, who at every moment tried to give God reasons why he should not be the one to free the Israelites, God reminded him of who his creator was because all of our faults and weaknesses are inconsequential to Him. And, Peter, a mere fisherman, Jesus saw Him as the rock on which He would build His Church.

Knowing their true self opens doors to wholeness in all the other areas of a person's life because the root of dysfunction is healed through their union with Christ. Once they are freed from the burden of performance under the Law, they can begin to focus on healing that needs to take place in the other pillars. The way we can support people is by reminding them of this reality that they are one with Christ. We can also help point them to the truth of God's Word. For example, Scripture repeatedly tells us that we should forgive others. Forgiveness is a very powerful and healing tool that allows us to let go of the hurt that is causing us pain. Inner healing ministry can be extremely beneficial to help walk people through not only forgiveness but also identifying thoughts that are not aligned with God's Word. Inner healing also helps the person connect more with the Holy Spirit and allow Him to be their comforter. It takes the focus off of us helping them and instead allows God to do the work. When a person heals from their trauma and let's go of past hurts, they begin to see how their mental, emotional, and relational situations begin to change in a positive way. When working with people in poverty, you may notice that some will operate from a position of distrust. Some people may have either been burned by people in their lives or a system, and so to cope they will keep themselves at a distance. Also, as we learned, people living in poverty are most at risk to experience adverse childhood events. Adverse childhood experiences can lead to depression, substance abuse, and suicide. When we carry deep emotional wounds, it not only impacts our mental health but can also cause troubles relationally and also manifest as physical illness. Therefore, we can help people practice a habit of forgiveness, which allows them to experience immense peace but also helps them better manage themselves emotionally. It may also help restore relationships that have been broken. In thinking about my own story, working through memories and forgiving allowed me to experience a higher degree of emotional wholeness which has been a game changer for me. I was healed of depression because I was able to partner with the Holy Spirit to heal each of my emotional wounds. Until I went through that process, I hadn't connected with how much of a hindrance my emotions were in my being successful in all areas of my life.

It is not enough to assume that these things will just happen on their own without discipleship. As a Church, we have to be intentional in helping not just the people who are in poverty to experience these truths, but every believer because life in abundance belongs to all of us. These pivotal first steps set the stage for the more practical aspects of wholeness such as financial, physical, and vocational. However, even these pillars are vines from the spiritual wholeness root. Without having an understanding of God or His kingdom, it makes it difficult to understand how our mindsets need to change about finances or that we have a purpose and were given the skills and talents in advance to achieve that purpose. Without knowing God's love for us and loving ourselves for our true selves, physical wholeness will be arduous. The other pillars also impact each other such as a lack of emotional wholeness can have an impact on the physical body, for example.

Admittedly, financial wholeness is something I personally struggle the most with because I remember what it was like to not have any food in the house and to see the overdue bills and eviction notices sitting on the kitchen counter. I remember the stress my mother felt worrying about how she was going to dig herself out of the hole of debt. This is where I developed a belief grounded in the fear of scarcity called poverty mindset. A poverty mindset is a belief that there will never be enough money or resources. This belief can lead to chronic stress and a feeling of lack of control over one's life. Poverty is not only a socioeconomic status; it is also a mindset that needs to be reset. Understanding this and the abundance of God is imperative if we are going to be carriers of peace and joy to this population. There are often generational cycles of poverty that can be broken if we can help one generation believe they can rise above their situation. We can teach people about money and how to manage it, but changing the mindset is what makes lasting change.

I believe the importance we place on money is one of the reasons God told us to give to anyone who asks (Luke 6:30-36). Nothing really belongs to us because every gift comes from God (James 1:17). Therefore, we are only stewards of what God has entrusted to us. We demonstrate a wealth mentality when we give freely, especially money, to those in need. It not only speaks of our generosity, but it is also a demonstration of who we are as a Kingdom nation. We are not only a holy nation, but a royal one. The Kingdom we belong to has a limitless supply of resources. There are times when I believed the lie that God wanted us to be poor and His Kingdom is limited in resources, but that is not so. In fact, there were many times that God blessed people financially beyond measure such as with Solomon. However, in the Church, we have hardwired the belief that to be poor is virtuous. This most likely comes from what Jesus said in Matthew 19:16-28 about it being difficult for a rich man to enter into Heaven. One thing to understand about this story isn't that the riches or possessions themselves cause difficulty for getting into Heaven, but as always, it is the heart behind it. Jesus wanted to know whether the young rich man would give up everything to follow Him. This is what we should be teaching in churches. We have to posture our hearts in such a way that we are willing to give everything if Jesus asks us to. This is especially difficult with money and possessions because there is a sense of security in knowing you have the financial means to live; however, it is this independence that takes away dependence on God as our provider. We need to break free of false security and remember God's truth: "And my God will supply every need of yours according to His riches in glory in Christ Jesus" (Phil. 4:19, ESV). We live in a world that is often not dependent on God, but on money, so to give it away whenever someone simply asks seems crazy. Our minds will fight this giving generously mindset and argue that we shouldn't do that. Just as we want to help those living in poverty change their habits around money, we must also change the way we think about it. If we develop a wealth mindset as the Church, we shift from a scarcity mindset to one that focuses on money being a tool used to invest. When we give money to those in poverty, it is a Kingdom investment and that will always have a good return.

What this chapter hinges on is our fervor around helping people not only know, but experience the Gospel by becoming one with Christ. It is this freedom that is indescribable, but necessary and available to all who choose to participate in it. The reality is that there is no self apart from Jesus. From the moment we accept Him, it is His Spirit that fills us to push out the parts of ourselves that are not of Him. As a Body, we are to shout from the rooftops this incredible gift to those who have yet to receive it, and remind each other daily of our identity so that we don't grow weary or become discouraged. Helping people discover their true selves removes the veil of ignorance of who they really are. In doing this, we can help them connect with the Holy Spirit and allow Him to reveal to them who they are as a new creation fully abiding in Christ.

Reflection

Read Parable of the Vine in John 15. Reflect and meditate on what it means to abide within the vine of Jesus. Spend some time with your eyes closed and ask Jesus to show you your unified, non-independent self.

Journal about what you see. Continue to meditate on this verse until you are able to see yourself in union with Jesus.

Prayer

Holy Spirit, I invite you to engage my imagination. As I sit here quietly mediating on John 15:4, you tell me to abide in you. Open the eyes of my imagination so that I might see myself in you. Please give me the revelation of being totally dependent and in union with you. Show me how I am returning to my independent self and help me to return to a state of abiding. Speak to me as I go through each day highlighting when I am not fully living in unity with you. In Jesus Name, Amen.

Chapter 10

"Here is what we seek: a compassion that can stand in awe at what the poor have to carry rather than stand in judgment at how they carry it."
— **Gregory Boyle**

Throughout this book, I have discussed various mindsets and practices that need to change in order to mobilize the people in our churches to meet the needs of our communities, and it all boils down to culture. However, in order to change culture, we first have to understand what it is and its purpose. When I use the word culture in this context, I refer to all the things that make a community or a group of people who they are. This includes the social norms and cues people use for the traditions they follow. It's the DNA that makes up the group and differentiates it from other groups. It is the unspoken norms that people follow without realizing why they are following them. While changing culture can be difficult, change can start with one person, and that person is you. You have been called to your church for such a time as this. In this chapter, I will lay out several steps I think are needed to get started down the path for change for your church. Some steps might be sequential and some may be parallel, but they all will help pave the way for a shift from Sunday Christian culture to an engaged, vibrant, Gospel-living congregation.

Step 1: Prepare

The most crucial part of this process is taking time to pray for the people in your church, in your community, and for yourself. Take time to listen to what God says and how He is directing you. The very first thing to do as you embark on your journey towards being moved by compassion leading to action is to wait on the Lord. Give yourself the space to listen to His voice. There is no plan too large that God won't provide for. Therefore, the first place to start is to spend time with Him and ask Him to increase your faith in the impossible. Root yourself in who He is and that He is a generous Father who wants to bless you and the work He has called you to do. It has been incredible to watch the Lord move in my own ministry. Every time I have had a need for my benevolence ministry, He has provided. I have found this to be true in my own ministry. For example, one year I had a $2500 benevolence budget, yet we were able to meet more than $6300 in needs because God provided the necessary resources. Above the financial needs that He provided for, we also received food and hygiene donations. I have learned to accept all donations because, without fail, someone would bring in a donation and soon after I would have a request for those items. Once I received a donation of towels and other household linens. In all honesty, when the person brought the donation in, I thought it was strange and wondered, "Who will need this?" But, I accepted it because I didn't want to reject this person's generosity. A couple weeks later, we were hosting a mobile food pantry and I was responsible for providing prayer and encouragement to those waiting in the cars. When I approached one of the vehicles, I met a man whose family had just lost everything in a house fire. He told me that he had received help with the bigger items such as a couch and kitchen table, but the small items like linens and kitchen utensils were hard to come by and he didn't have the means to purchase them. I was able to give him the linens and towels that had been donated. Another time, I received a call from a family saying they were in dire need of food. At that time, I wasn't sure how that need would be met so I just asked the Lord to help me. The next day, Sunday morning, a woman approached me before our church service to ask me if I needed food because she had a large food donation that she felt like she should bring to me. Not only was I able to feed that one family with that donation, but it was enough food to feed five more families that needed assistance. Over and over God has demonstrated His generosity, but in our humanness, we can lack faith or trust that He will provide even despite the many examples of His faithfulness to us.

For such a long time many in the Church have stopped believing in the supernatural. Sometimes I read Scripture and think about what the Church would look like if we got a revelation about what Jesus was saying was possible for us. He said that all things are possible with God (Matt. 19:26). He said that while He had done great things, we would do greater (John 14:12-14). I long for a Church that has such radical faith in the impossible that nothing deters them from accomplishing what God has called us to do. To think you can transform a city takes an exorbitant amount of faith and people will think that you are crazy for having such an unachievable goal. Remember, we need to become comfortable with people thinking we are a little crazy because we believe in the impossible. You have to be firm in the vision that God has set before you. Don't let anyone deter you from it—be obsessed. Believe me, people will try to tell you all the reasons something won't work, especially because this kind of radical love, generosity, and service has been nearly absent from the Church for a long time. So, before embarking on this journey and during it, be sure to be listening for the Holy Spirit as He prepares you for what is ahead because transforming cities is Kingdom work. Fostering a heart of compassion in churches and mobilizing them to do the work of the Kingdom is unnerving for the Enemy. He will launch attacks at you in order to discourage you, prevent you from moving forward, and to deplete your faith. I notice that whenever I am about to break through a barrier or a milestone in ministry, conflict in my life pops up in order to get me to focus my attention on that versus what God needs me to do. This is the time when I need to rest in the Lord more than ever and remember what Jesus said, "I have told you all this so that you may have peace in me. Here on earth you will have many trials and sorrows. But take heart, because I have overcome the world" (John 16:33, NLT).

Another point of advice to you is to allow the Lord to strengthen you before and during the ministry He has called you to do. Take time for self-care and do not let the work of ministry negatively impact your family and relationships. This is another area the enemy will attack. Set healthy boundaries between yourself and ministry. You are not the one "saving" the city: Jesus is. He can work through others when you are "off duty."

Step 2: Work with Your Church Leadership

Getting things done, in any organization, is much easier when you have the support of your leadership. It is crucial that all levels of leadership are engaged when making change. If the decision makers in your church are not on board, you need to go back and ask the Lord for direction and also to honestly reflect on your assignment and where He has positioned you. It could be the right idea, but the wrong time. Be confident that He will guide you and open up the right doors for you when needed. With that said, find the things that your leaders are willing to buy into and start there.

Everett Rogers, in his book *Diffusion Innovation*, wrote about a model he calls the Rogers' adoption curve, which illustrates the willingness of a person within a group to accept new ideas and/or change. It looks like this:

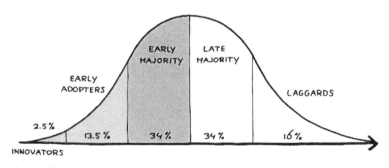

photo credit: Jurgen Appelo

You can see that people fall on various points of the spectrum in terms of willingness to accept change. Most people are within the early to late majority, while on the left of the spectrum are the innovators and early adopters who are polar opposites of the laggards. Each group on the spectrum can have some characteristics that give us insight into how they think about change. In the Characteristics: Innovators to Laggards figure, the characteristics of each adopter and how they approach change are listed. Knowing these characteristics can help us know how to best interact and communicate with the different types of adopters.

Characteristics: Innovators to Laggards

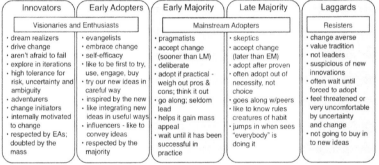

Innovators	Early Adopters	Early Majority	Late Majority	Laggards
Visionaries and Enthusiasts		Mainstream Adopters		Resisters
• dream realizers • drive change • aren't afraid to fail • explore in iterations • high tolerance for risk, uncertainty and ambiguity • adventurers • change initiators • internally motivated to change • respected by EAs; doubted by the mass	• evangelists • embrace change • self-efficacy • like to be first to try, use, engage, buy • try our new ideas in careful way • inspired by the new • like integrating new ideas in useful ways • influencers - like to convey ideas • respected by the majority	• pragmatists • accept change (sooner than LM) • deliberate • adopt if practical - • adopt if practical - weigh out pros & cons; think it out • go along; seldom lead • helps it gain mass appeal • wait until it has been successful in practice	• skeptics • accept change (later than EM) • adopt after proven • often adopt out of necessity, not choice • goes along w/peers • like to know rules • creatures of habit • jumps in when sees "everybody" is doing it	• change averse • value tradition • not leaders • suspicious of new innovations • often wait until forced to adopt • feel threatened or very uncomfortable by uncertainty and change • not going to buy in to new ideas

Characteristics Image by The Center for Creative Emergence 2011
Main Sources: Diffusion of Innovation by Everett Rogers
Crossing the Chasm by Geoffrey Moore

Innovators are people who are excited about new things who don't worry about whether things are going to work out or not because they are natural risk takers. You probably already know who they are. They are the people who are your biggest cheerleaders. They are excited about change and are usually flexible when change is happening. Change invigorates them. Early Adopters are also risk takers, but they tend to be a little more cautious and typically like to try things before they commit to changing. They are usually leaders in their own right and are people who typically have influence. Early Majority and Late Majority are people who tend to be less risky. The Early Majority are typically those who will want to be involved once a new idea has become more formalized and established. Late Majority folks could go either way. Some of them may be on board once they see the fruit of the labors of all those who got on board early. But, then there are the Laggards. The Laggards are typically those who are traditionalists. They have seen a lot of new ideas start and fizzle out, so they will most likely be critical of any type of change.

Thankfully, there are strategies you can employ to address the needs of each person in the corresponding groups. Innovators and Early Adopters will be the people who want to get on board with what God is doing in your community first. They will become your change agents that get excited and tell everyone else how great this change is. For the people in the Early and Late Majority, it is all about communication. They want to know what is in it for them. It is important for you to help them see the benefits and the meaning that the change you are proposing has for them. In my opinion, the Laggards get a bad rap because they tend to dig their heels in and won't budge. However, I have seen that people in this group often do better when they are involved in any change early on because their concerns are addressed early in the process. Not involving them, even if it might be challenging to do so, will help you later on when the change is ready to be implemented because likely, they will already have accepted the idea. Laggards are usually the people who are the toughest to get on board. They are your critics and want to see the effort is going to pay off and the outcome is going to be good before they get involved. Find someone who has influence so that as things progress they can help draw in the other Laggards. Otherwise, as harsh as it may sound, don't get stuck in the cycle of spinning your wheels on a group that doesn't want to participate; instead focus on the other 80% who are invested in what you are doing. Just remember before you do anything, ask the Holy Spirit to pave the way and give you a strategy for how to begin moving HIS plan for your church forward.

Above all, the best way to start a movement and change culture is to begin with yourself. If you have trouble getting your leadership on board with a big idea, start with a small one. Model the behavior or the change that you would like to see in your church. Most people will begin to see the fruit of what God is asking you to do and begin to get involved. If you are reading this book, you are probably in that Innovator or Early Adopter part of the curve. If your leadership team is on the other side of the curve, be patient with them. Pray for them. Ask them to read this book. Sometimes the first step in changing is simply gaining the knowledge needed to open our minds to a new perspective.

Step 3: Connect the Dots

When I first took on the role of Outreach Director at my local church, I started to do research. I wanted to understand what the specific problems in my community were. I began by searching the Internet for public sources of data and information available on municipal, state, and federal websites. Then, I started meeting with local agencies to learn about the needs of the community. It was also a way to connect with area leaders or those doing similar work. I met with our food bank, school principals, non-profit directors, and other church leaders. I wasn't sure at the time where God was leading me, but I knew the value of knowing people and having a network. It was during this time my prayer focused on asking the Lord what exactly He wanted me to focus on. He responded and led me to a mobile home park that was located across the street from my church. This mobile home park became our church's metron, or sphere of influence — our local mission field. The park itself was largely hidden from view as it was situated behind a strip mall. I called it the invisible neighborhood because driving by you would never notice it was there. I found out through my research that they were experiencing issues related to hunger, economic instability, and poor health at more than twice the rate when compared to our county. Additionally, their rent was twice the average in the county and state. I also found out that the people who lived there were ineligible for certain government benefits simply because they lived in a mobile home park. Further, half the homes had school-age children and many of those children were living with grandparents. I told anyone who would listen about the problems those living in this mobile home park were experiencing. In doing this, something interesting happened— people not only listened, they began to care.

Most people aren't aware of the issues in their community and if they are, they might not know what to do about them. There is a lot to be said about the power of the Hawthorne effect, which is simply a phenomenon that describes how people change by simply becoming aware of something else. People also connect with stories. You may want to consider putting together a schedule of speakers who are either knowledgeable about the problems occurring in your local mission field or who have experienced it. You can determine what types of things, activities, or topics you can begin to integrate to build awareness about the issues in your community. You may also want to consider having local organizations talk to your congregation about issues or initiatives they have underway. It could be as simple as using your church Facebook page or special group to start educating and giving a space for awareness and discussions. These types of things will help your congregation and team gain knowledge and also start to draw connections with why their church is going to be working to address those needs in your determined local mission field.

Step 4: Engage with your Tribe

When I first began ministry, God was so good to me. Before I even knew what was ahead He surrounded me with people who would be honest with me and be a source of encouragement. On multiple occasions as I was learning to work through the emotionality of some things I had been challenged with, one of those people would send me a card or give me encouragement. Some even in the form of prophetic words. I have cherished these people and often sought out their counsel and support. I am especially thankful for my husband and children because they have played a significant role in supporting me. They made sacrifices when I have had to go on a ministry call or to prepare for an event. All of these people understand what it takes to build the Kingdom here on Earth and have given so much to that cause. They have also spoken and invested in the vision God gave me for city transformation and eliminating poverty, and, most importantly, they have been marvelous intercessors and prayer warriors.

You will need a tribe too. You need people who can be close to you that you can be vulnerable with such as a spouse or trusted friend. Then, ask your prayer ministry team or those with a gift for intercession to begin praying for you and the vision God has given you for your church. Ask the Lord to show you who should be on your team. This will most likely be the people who will work with you to develop this vision and make it happen. Each will have their own gifting. Your job as a leader is to help them connect with those gifts and how God wants to use their gifts on this team. Once you have assembled your team, give them the opportunity to pray about and contribute ideas for realizing the vision. Also, this seems obvious, but oftentimes we get caught up in doing "work" that we forget to get to know our team. Be purposeful in getting to know them and to have fun together. Before you embark on your own journey of community impact, find ways to serve together like at a local soup kitchen or food pantry. Building strong relationships within your team is the best gift you can give them and yourself.

Step 5: Start Small

One thing I had to continually remind myself of is that I didn't have to build this perfect program before I could begin. I had to just start somewhere. My suggestion to you is that you find a way to start small. Make that one thing really great and then move on to the next thing. The first year in our local ministry was simply about building a presence in the community. We did things like hosting a community day, pancake breakfasts, and family movie nights. We were fortunate that the management of the mobile home park was welcoming and wanted to work with us, which allowed us to use their clubhouse to host events. We wanted to show the community they were worth the investment of our time and resources and that we wanted to meet them where they were: on their own turf. This gives them the respect they deserve. Even Jesus had to go out amongst the people. They came to him once they recognized the importance of His message.

Another approach we decided to take during the first year was to intentionally not make the events "churchy." Many people may be jaded by the church and Christians in particular. We still had subtle signage that said our church name on it, and if we did giveaways we would include scriptures with the prizes or select books with a biblical message. But we never preached at them. Our goal was to simply build a relationship with them so they could trust us and the message we represented.

Step 6: Integrate

What I have found is that there are a lot of ways to get involved at most churches. Most churches that are small to medium in size could have troubles with drawing from the same pool of volunteers. Find ways to integrate outreach activities into each ministry and event at your church. Instill a culture of outreach being every person's responsibility. Partner with the other pastors or department heads in your church to brainstorm ways this can happen. For example, if your children's department is hosting an event at Christmas, partner with them to ask each attendee to bring a hygiene product. Schools are often in need of those items as hygiene products aren't usually available through food pantries and community resources. You can pick anything that aligns with the vision that God has given you for your church and local community. Many churches host events for Mother's Day or around Christmas time. You could create a theme around the event that highlights a need in the community such as human trafficking or collecting baby items.

Step 7: Build a Team

Spend time praying about who God wants on your team. You don't just want people who will agree with everything you say because having someone who will challenge you in a constructive way can be a great asset. Putting a team together may sound easy. You just pick a few people that you like or recognize are talented and put them in a room and it just works, right? That might make for a great party, but definitely not for a team. Each person should be selected because they have a skill or talent that makes them appropriate and beneficial for the team. Some thought should be put into what skills and gifting you might need to accomplish the vision you have for your local mission field. For example, if you want to start a community garden, you will need people who are skilled at gardening, but may also need someone who is gifted in administration who can make sure logistical details are managed such as scheduling volunteers and purchasing supplies. You may also need someone who is talented in building relationships that can work with the people in the community to gain participation with the garden.

A great way to understand the skills and talents is to ask people in your church or those interested in being on your team to take a spiritual gifts test. You may also want to consider asking your church to take a skills assessment. This would be helpful as projects and programs start up you can identify what skills are needed and who would be best suited to help. There may be people in your church who are business owners who have connections within the community, are craftsmen, or are gifted in cooking. Ultimately, just as when the first tabernacle was built and the skilled workers were already in place, God has likely already brought the people needed to accomplish this vision to your church or at the very least will be sending them. Asking Him Who He wants to include on your team should be part of your process. Over time as you build relationships in the community for which you are ministering, you may ask someone who lives in that neighborhood to join your team. They will not only bring a new perspective, but also may be someone who can connect easily with others living in the neighborhood.

Step 8: Integrate Coproduction
Coproduction is about getting people together to tackle problems collaboratively. Let's say you discover that your neighborhood has food insecurity. You could think of several ways on your own on how to address that. However, you might not have the experience and knowledge that others might bring to the table. Therefore, you might want to consider hosting a brainstorming session with your team, the local food pantry, and business owners who want to invest

137

in charitable work in the community. Coproduction is the process in which all these things we have talked about in this chapter come together. You have a cohesive team with diverse gifts, talents, skills, and experiences who come together for a common purpose: meeting the needs of those living in poverty.

Compassion in Action

The Book of Acts opens with Jesus on the Mount of Transfiguration, where he instructs the Apostles to wait on the Holy Spirit so they might be baptized in the Spirit and then He says, "But you will receive power when the Holy Spirit comes upon you. And you will be my witnesses, telling people about me everywhere—in Jerusalem, throughout Judea, Samaria, and to the ends of the earth" (Acts 1:8, NLT). Jesus gives us a framework for how we should approach building an outreach program which isn't a program at all, it is a culture where every person in your church takes responsibility for sharing the Gospel and serving the community. Jesus tells us to start where we are, and then begin to increase the territory we cover. What if each church approached developing this culture at their church? Start where they are and then spread to international missions? Imagine the territory we could cover. The problem is that our current traditional model is to start with international missions and most never really get invested in local missions. It has become easy for us to be comfortable writing a check so that we check the "we do missions" box. Doing missions this way doesn't require us to "roll up our sleeves and get our hands dirty," but it gives us a feeling of doing good in the world and spreading the Gospel wherever that check ends up. However, each and every one of us is supposed to be spreading the Gospel right where we are by loving people. It is time that we flip the script and begin to ask the Lord what is our assignment in the location He has placed us, instead of thinking that the job of evangelism belongs to people living in Africa. International missions are critical to spreading the Gospel. I have friends who are missionaries and I am thankful for the good work they are doing. When it is time for your church to spread its reach to international

138

missions, God will provide the means and may even raise up a missionary from your own congregation or town for you to support.

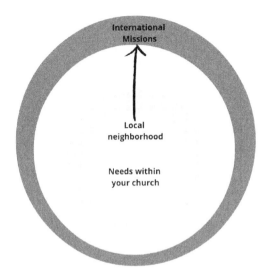

In Chapter 8, I talked about visualizing growing your outreach program being represented by a bullseye. Your influence starts first within your church, your local community, and spreads from there.

Each ring in the diagram represents a new sphere of influence, with the center being your individual church congregation. Jesus said, "A new command I give you: Love one another. As I have loved you, so you must love one another. By this everyone will know that you are my disciples, if you love one another" (John 13:34-35, NIV). Throughout the Gospels, we see Jesus caring for his flock. This is what we are to model. When we take care of and love one another, the world will know that we are truly disciples of Jesus.

Remember it is also important that you have a robust benevolence process because as you begin to spread your influence of outreach, you will find that calls from people not within your church will begin to increase. When this started happening in my own church,

I attributed it to how God thought it was time for us to begin facing outward. It is important for you to spend some time refining this process and establishing sources of financial support, as once you begin receiving more calls any hiccups in your process will be confounded.

While benevolence, or charitable giving, is important—it is more accurately described as crisis control. While it is important to give generously to those in need, we should help them get to a healthier place so they aren't stuck in the loop of relying on the Church. We have to remember to help them rely on Jesus first, as He is the source of our wholeness. We must get great at helping individuals before we can think about helping populations. In order to help people in poverty, we have to be willing to step into their shoes and meet them where they are in that moment. Be compassionate with those who need help by understanding that if they are coming to you they could be feeling desperate, hopeless, scared, and/or vulnerable. I meet with everyone I help in one capacity or another because developing a relationship is more important. Many people by the time they get to me are overwhelmed and emotionally bankrupt. We can help them by offering spiritual support and then managing the practical needs that are presenting as a crisis. But, the question becomes: How do we help them to not return to this place of crisis again? The first step, to quote Steven Covey, is "seek first to understand." Instead of focusing on what you think they need to change, take time to understand what you might not know about that person first. Put aside judgements and don't analyze all the decisions they made to get to that moment. Be diligent about listening. Remember that they are likely stuck in a system that heaps challenges and barriers on them. Is it unreasonable they would subscribe to the belief they should just accept their fate or that their life will never be any better? Instead help them remember what it is like to dream and believe in themselves.

At the end of the day, outreach is about people and helping them experience the love of Jesus. A very wise friend and colleague told me that people usually have enough people telling them what they should and shouldn't do and there is also no shortage of people in their lives telling them their faults. He said, instead, be that person who is always there to accept them with open arms and be willing to patiently love them while they figure out their own way. This is the way that God loves us—He is patient, kind, gentle, and He trusts, hopes, keeps no records of wrongs, and doesn't condemn; instead He protects us and never gives up on us. This is what a suffering world needs to be whole.

Thank You

I hope you have enjoyed reading *Moved by Compassion: Mobilizing Your Local Church to Transform Your City*. If you are feeling inspired to make change in your local community, be part of the movement by joining the *Moved by Compassion* Facebook group: https://www.facebook.com/groups/movedbycompassion. You will gain **FREE** access to teachings and become part of a body of believers that is passionate about transforming communities.

 As an author, speaker, and community advocate, Jamie Lindsay is compelled by the Father's love for people. Her passion is empowering the local church to tangibly express God's love and effectively share the Gospel with those in need through their radical giving and practical acts of service.

As founder and CEO of Moved by Compassion Academy, Jamie's mission is to equip churches so that believers are empowered and mobilized to meet every need in their community. Jamie's unique perspective combines working as an outreach director and continuous improvement coach with her background in public health to bring a unique approach to developing church outreach programs.

As a Director of Outreach at her local church, Jamie and her team worked with individuals who are experiencing financial difficulties or facing homelessness. She also helped develop relationships with a local elementary school to develop a mentorship program for at-risk children. Additionally, she has helped her church connect with a local neighborhood, where they work to understand the needs of the residents and provide programming to support those needs. She has worked to build bridges between their work in the neighborhood and local resources and employers to better help those living in the community.

When not changing the world one city at a time, Jamie and her family enjoy spending time outdoors kayaking, biking, and just relaxing at the beach.

ANOINTED
PUBLISHING

Printed in Great Britain
by Amazon